A Garden of Virtues

A Garden of Virtues

A Bouquet of Stories About Timeless Virtues

☙

Including biblical passages and essays by
Martin Luther, Charles Dickens,
Nathaniel Hawthorne, Thomas à Kempis,
Billy Graham, Louisa May Alcott,
Hans Christian Andersen, Abraham Lincoln,
Francis of Assisi, and many other
inspirational writers.

GRAMERCY BOOKS
New York

This 1998 edition is published by Gramercy Books,
a division of Random House Value Publishing, Inc.,
201 East 50th Street, New York, New York 10022,
by arrangement with Abingdon Press.

Gramercy Books® and design are registered trademarks of
Random House Value Publishing, Inc.

Random House
New York • Toronto • London • Sydney • Auckland
http://www.randomhouse.com/

Printed and bound in the United States of America

A CIP catalog record for this book is available from the Library of Congress.

A Garden of Virtues / ISBN 0-517-20282-4

8 7 6 5 4 3 2 1

Contents

LOVE AND CHARITY

TEMPERANCE

From Virtues to Values and Back Again

Character has become a lost commodity. In fact, it is so lost that we find it hard even to define what it means. In earlier days, character was what you had when you unflinchingly lived by the commonly held virtues of society. But character vanishes when there are no virtues. America, and in some respects the church, has lost its sense of virtue.

I hadn't even heard the word *virtues* for a long time until William Bennett published his book by that title. I remember purchasing a copy when it first came out and saying to the young, trendy, intellectual-looking clerk, "This will probably be a bestseller." To which he replied, "I hope not."

His reply was enigmatic to me until I read a fascinating book by Gertrude Himmelfarb entitled *The Demoralization of Society*. She traces the intentional, philosophical shift away from the concept of *virtue* to the now commonly accepted term, *value*. Virtue relates to behavior that is morally best, that which conforms to a common moral authority. A value, on the other hand, relates to a personal set of preferences that I as an individual have determined as the standard by which I will measure my choices and my accountability.

Through the past several decades, we have seen the steady erosion of a common moral authority in America. In the past, this agreement to the basic moral codes of Moses and Christ was the standard by which we all were measured. Cultural absolutes gave us targets to aim at. The social order honored integrity, hard work, loyalty, faithfulness to family, respect for authority, sexual purity, selfless compassion, and other morally constructive commodities. These were absolutes. They were our virtues.

Recently, however, such virtues have been marked for extinction by those who speak so powerfully through music, movies, TV dramas, sitcoms, and media commentaries. Relativists have also flooded our educational system, telling our children that because there are no moral absolutes, they can choose their own set of values by which to live.

Few people seem to link the rise in violence, crime, disease, disorientation, the breakdown of the family, and the increase in despair to this shift from virtues to values. But it's hard to ignore the fact that we have lost much as a country since we became so "enlightened," since we lost our virtue.

Even more troublesome, this shift from virtues to values is evident in the mindset of many Christians. We talk about the importance of values. We verbalize our concern for family values and the return of morality to America. But I often get the impression that we count these to be *our* values, choices that *we* have made from a range of available options.

George Barna notes that in a recent survey of Americans, 71 percent said they don't believe in absolutes. What is shocking is that 40 percent of evangelical Christians don't either.

I sometimes hear Christians say things like, "Well, I believe it's wrong for me, but I can't say it's wrong for everyone else." Whenever we say that, we are talking values, not virtues. That kind of thinking neutralizes the compelling power of righteousness. It disables us from calling our children and our culture to a clear understanding of God's standard of behavior, by which we all will be measured.

Our moral authority is nothing less than God Himself. He is true, just, loving, merciful, pure, faithful, and benevolent. His nature establishes the absolute standard.

The qualities that comprise His character are not simply things that comprise *our* values. They are the essence of what is correct for all of society, for all mankind. They are the measures of character, respectability, stability, and safety.

If we His people lose our sense of absolute virtue, we will lose not only our character, but also our opportunity to bring a healing voice to a hurting world. We will compromise the very nature of His correct and changeless glory reflected through our lives.

May we instead be people who unashamedly cling to the absolutes of God's character and who by our own lives call others to virtue again.

Joseph M. Stowell

Let Virtue Be Your Aim

Whatever be thy lot on earth,
    Thy mission here below,
Though Fame may wreathe her laurels fair,
    Around your youthful brow,
If you would rise from earthly things,
    And win a deathless name,
Let all your ways be just and right—
    Let virtue be your aim.

Though cherished friends may traitor prove,
    Their kindness all depart,
And leave a mournful spell around
    Thy sad and bleeding heart;
Though you may oft be scorned by men,
    Or those who bear the name,
Let all your ways be just and right—
    Let virtue be your aim.

C. Jillson

FAITH

As Paul underlined to the Hebrews, we are surrounded by a great cloud of witnesses to the faith, even from the beginning of time. When we speak of having faith in something, we mean that we believe it with our whole hearts. As the patriarchs believed in the one Lord, so we have faith in God and in his son, Jesus Christ. We trust God and Jesus and we will be loyal to them, no matter what trials we must suffer. We believe that God and Jesus will remain faithful and loyal to us, too. We place our trust in them, knowing that we can rely on them through good times and bad.

Now faith is the assurance of things hoped for, the conviction of things not seen.

Hebrews 11:1 NRSV

EVIDENCE OF THINGS NOT SEEN

How limited our lives would be if we could be blessed only by things we can fully understand—things we can see with our eyes and "prove" with our reason. Faith should never be unreasonable, but it must constantly go beyond reason if we are to live fully and abundantly. We are all blessed by a mother's love long before we can begin to understand it; we never can completely describe, see, weigh, or measure such a precious gift. There is in it something of the nature of a loving God. It goes far beyond scientific description; we simply accept it and give thanks. Most of the really important aspects of a good life are outside and beyond the realm of materialistic observation. When my wife tells me that she loves me, I am glad that I don't need to ask her to prove it. I am blessed and satisfied with the evidence—her loyalty, a loving touch, a smile.

Have you ever wondered about the ability of blossoms to put so much fragrance into the springtime air without seeming to be diminished by what they give? A rose can give a sweet smell to an entire room for a long time and never seem a bit smaller for what it has given of itself. I suppose there is a scientific explanation for this abundance, but I am glad that I do not need to understand it before I can appreciate it. I don't have to see it to believe it.

Most of us believe in the goals of our career and life work long before we see these goals accomplished, and our belief helps us to bring them into being. The scientist seeking a cure for disease or the explanation for a natural event believes in what he or she searches for before discovering and seeing it. Believing leads us to the discovery of new truth. It is belief in what lies beyond the horizon that leads us on so that someday we may see it.

Don Ian Smith

Light Shining out of Darkness

God moves in a mysterious way
   His wonders to perform;
He plants his footsteps in the sea,
   And rides upon the storm.

Deep in unfathomable mines
   Of never-failing skill
He treasures up his bright designs
   And works his sovereign will.

Ye fearful saints, fresh courage take:
   The clouds ye so much dread
Are big with mercy, and shall break
   In blessings on your head.

Judge not the Lord by feeble sense,
   But trust him for his grace;
Behind a frowning providence
   He hides a smiling face.

His purposes will ripen fast,
   Unfolding every hour;
The bud may have a bitter taste,
   But sweet will be the flower.

Blind unbelief is sure to err,
   And scan his work in vain;
God is his own interpreter,
   And he will make it plain.

William Cowper
1731–1800

THE WONDER TREE

One day in the springtime, Prince Solomon was sitting under the palm trees in the royal gardens, when he saw the Prophet Nathan walking near.

"Nathan," said the Prince, "I would see a wonder."

The Prophet smiled. "I had the same desire in the days of my youth," he replied.

"And was it fulfilled?" asked Solomon.

"A Man of God came to me," said Nathan, "having a pomegranate seed in his hand. 'Behold,' he said, 'what will become of this.' Then he made a hole in the ground, and planted the seed, and covered it over. When he withdrew his hand the clods of earth opened, and I saw two small leaves coming forth. But scarcely had I beheld them, when they joined together and became a small stem wrapped in bark; and the stem grew before my eyes, —and it grew thicker and higher and became covered with branches.

"I marveled, but the Man of God motioned me to be silent. 'Behold,' said, he, 'new creations begin.'

"Then he took water in the palm of his hand, and sprinkled the branches three times, and, lo! the branches were covered with green leaves, so that a cool shade spread above us, and the air was filled with perfume.

"'From whence come this perfume and this shade?' cried I.

"'Dost thou not see,' he answered, 'these crimson flowers bursting from among the leaves, and hanging in clusters?'

"I was about to speak, but a gentle breeze moved the leaves, scattering the petals of the flowers around us. Scarcely had the falling flowers reached the ground when I saw ruddy pomegranates hanging beneath the leaves of the tree, like almonds on Aaron's rod. Then the Man of God left me, and I was lost in amazement."

"Where is he, this Man of God?" asked Prince Solomon eagerly. "What is his name? Is he still alive?"

"Son of David," answered Nathan, "I have spoken to thee of a vision."

When the Prince heard this he was grieved to the heart. "How couldst thou deceive me thus?" he asked.

But the Prophet replied: "Behold in thy father's gardens thou mayest daily see the unfolding of wonder trees. Doth not this same miracle happen to the fig, the date, and the pomegranate? They spring from the earth, they put out branches and leaves, they flower, they fruit, — not in a moment, perhaps, but in months and years, — but canst thou tell the difference betwixt a minute, a month, or a year in the eyes of Him with whom one day is as a thousand years, and a thousand years as one day?"

Friedrich Adolph Krummacher (Adapted)

JUSTIFICATION BY FAITH

Why are we justified by faith? Because by faith we grasp Christ's righteousness, by which alone we are reconciled with God. Yet you could not grasp this without at the same time grasping sanctification. When Christ reconciles a person with God, he also wants to make them holy.

Indeed justification and sanctification are joined together by an eternal and unbreakable bond, so that those whom Christ saves, he also makes wise—those whom he justifies, he also sanctifies.

Let us dwell on the matter of sanctification. Do you wish to be saved by Christ? Then you must become like Christ, because he saves people by enabling them to imitate him. Jesus saves us by giving his life for us. And this in turn means that we must fully participate in his life, as part of his body. It is not that we must become holy, in order to be saved, for salvation can never be achieved by our own efforts. Rather it is that in saving us Christ makes us holy.

John Calvin
from *The Institutes*
1509–1564

FAITH AND WORKS

Faith is not the human achievement that people often call faith.
. . . If a person hears the gospel, and immediately gets busy with
various good works, he may by his own effort create a feeling in
his heart which he describes as faith. But this feeling can never
penetrate the depths of the heart, nor will it bear fruit in true selfless love.

Faith is wrought not by us, but by God. It transforms us, so that
we are born anew. It kills the old Adam, making us altogether different . . . in heart and mind and spirit. Faith is busy and active,
impelling us to do good works. It does not need to count the cost
of those good works, but simply gets on with them. Those without
faith may talk and talk, both about faith and good works, but
remain ignorant of both.

Faith is a living, daring trust in God. A person with faith would
stake his whole life on the grace of God. This knowledge and confidence in God makes men glad and bold and joyful in all their
dealings, both with God and with his creatures. A person with
faith is willing to love all people, to serve and suffer for all people,
praising God in everything. Thus it is impossible to separate good
works from faith, just as it is impossible to separate the heat from
the light of a fire.

Martin Luther
1483–1546

22

VINCE'S STORY

Vince was not a man of dreams. His shoe repair shop was certainly not a dream. It was at the bottom of a stairwell, recessed into the sidewalk of a city street which was mostly vacant these days. Once, when Vince was learning the trade from Vincent Popich, Sr., the street was busy. Apartments were the homes of middle class families, stores did a good business, and life on this street was going somewhere. Not today. Few people walked the sidewalks above his shop. In spite of the condition of the neighborhood, his business did well. People drove in from the suburbs to get their shoes fixed. They had no choice. Suburban shoemakers were rare. So Vince stayed in the old building. He had a room upstairs, so it was handy.

Life for Vince was lived on this street, between the shop, Tiny's Cafe three storefronts toward the avenue, and his apartment upstairs. He saw few people. The customers didn't stay long, looking tense and anxious to get back into the car. Besides them, his only worry was the stairwell. It seemed crazy to him because the street was almost always empty but it was hard to keep the stairwell clear of people. Mornings he would leave his apartment, walk down the front stairs, go around to the side and check the stairwell before descending to open his shop. Drunks slept there. Vince supposed that they were harmless but he was afraid of them. When he found someone sleeping there, he would walk around to the back of the stairwell, lean over the rail, and yell. That rarely worked. Then he would drop cans or whatever he could find on the street. He didn't aim to hurt them. Just wake them up. Once a man woke up swinging. Vince was glad to be clear of the stairwell. He never stopped to think about what he would do if he was the one being awakened by being hit on the head with a can.

Then there were the kids. Vince couldn't figure out where they came from. No kids lived in his building. Wherever they came from, he wished they would stay there. They could figure out all kinds of reasons to come down the stairs. They would hide down there, chase the balls that constantly found their way down, and hang on the railing. The more he chased them away, the more they came.

Vince was not a man of dreams. He lived each day awake and slept each night. That was enough. But last night he had a dream. At least he thought it was a dream. As he opened the door to the shop, the stairwell was clear today, he remembered. He'd had an angel beside his bed. He believed in angels although he had not been in a church for years. When he was younger and his parents took him to church, he used to squint at the angels on the windows and pretend that they were moving. He liked the story of the angel visiting Mary. As a child he had expected such a visit someday. Once it seemed to Vince that he was special and that such a visit was entirely reasonable. Now, when he had given up on angels for years, an angel had visited his room. At first he thought he was dying. Then he decided that he was dreaming.

The angel spoke a simple promise. "The Lord himself is going to visit your shop, Vince. Be ready for him."

Vince called out to wake himself from the dream but he was already sitting on the side of the bed. He sat there a moment, noticed the early light of dawn entering through the one window and decided to head down to Tiny's for an early breakfast. He decided to forget the dream.

He could not. It stayed with him as he continued the routine of opening his shop. He checked the opening balance in the cash register. The idea of God seemed real to him again. He examined the shoes on his "to-do" shelf, looking for the oldest order to start first. The dream made him feel special. But it was just a dream. Vince decided to enjoy the momentary pleasant feeling and forget about it.

In the middle of a leather resole job, the world entered his doorstep in the form of a basketball. This one hit the window, startling him before it settled in the corner. *I'm going to lose a window someday,* he concluded as he headed to the door to grab the ball. When they hit the window, he would grab the balls and keep them in his back room. He had two shipping crates full of an assortment of stray balls. Just as he opened the door, a young girl with a green parka and no mittens bounded down the stairs. She spotted Vince when she was about halfway down but her momentum carried her past him to the bottom of the steps. Vince stepped out and she was trapped. Their eyes met for a moment and then Vince looked downward quickly. He simply could not bear to confront the fear in her eyes. He spotted the ball, reached past her to pick it up, and then handed it to her. She hesitated at first, not daring to reach toward this man she feared. Vince then surprised himself. He handed her the ball, opened the door, and said in a voice that sounded foreign to him, "Get your friends and come back to my shop. I have something for you." She slipped by him, making the escape which moments ago looked impossible, and ran up the stairs.

"Please come back with your friends," he called after her. "You won't be in trouble." Vince shut the door behind him and went back to leather soles. He knew that he wanted the kids to come back, he just didn't understand why. He didn't have time to wonder. He heard a rap on the window that opened to the staircase. She must have needed the strength of numbers because she now stood in the little stairwell with more than a half a dozen children. They stood and looked in at him. He stood and looked out. Then Vince turned to the back room. He slid a shipping crate filled with balls, from tennis to basketball, out and turned to get the other. With both crates in place he motioned for the kids to come in.

His first young friend stepped in and Vince bounced a basketball her way. She passed it back and instantly there appeared an assembly line of recovered balls. Baseball, football, koosh ball, and more. One by one they passed from Vince to the hands of their original owners or in some cases, the children of the original owners. This affair continued without a word until the sidewalk was covered with balls. He handed his young friend the remaining two baseball caps and a tennis racquet and then spoke his words. "Now be gone."

She turned back towards him as she left the shop and said simply, "Thank you." There were no promises and no explanations. As the door swung shut he heard the sound of balls, bouncing. Vince enjoyed himself as he continued to sole and resole throughout the day. He listened for bouncing balls.

The next morning he found another sleeper. He stood at the top of the stairs and shouted. It worked this time. The man stood up immediately and looked up at Vince. Fear. There was the same fear in his eyes that Vince had seen in the little girl.

"You look cold," Vince said in a voice that he did not recognize as his own. "Come in and have some warm coffee," he continued. "I've got some doughnuts." He opened the door and guided the sleeper to the only chair in the shop. The man moved the chair closer to the heat vent. Now that he had him in the shop Vince didn't know what to do next. The man solved the problem. "Got anything else to eat?" he said as he finished his doughnut. Vince had no other food but he had an idea.

"I'll write a note for Tiny down the street. Take it to him and I'll pay your bill when I get there for lunch," Vince said, feeling happy to have figured out a way to get the man out of his shop again. He quickly scribbled a note to Tiny, signed it, and watched the man as he ascended the staircase.

The days of deep winter were poor for business so Vince busied himself cleaning the shop. As he worked, it occurred to him that it was almost as if he were getting ready for company. Then he remembered the dream again. *"Whatever you do to the least of these, you do to me,"* he recalled from somewhere in his past. *"That's it,"* he concluded. *"That is what the dream meant. The sleeper and the kids. That's what they were to me."* Vince shook his head and sat down. *"Isn't that just like religion,"* he continued. *"God himself comes to see you and it costs you money."* He returned to his cleaning, wishing that no one else would come to his shop today.

His wish was granted. He spent the rest of the day alone. He sat alone at Tiny's and went home to be alone. Sleep was a mercy that night. An interrupted mercy. Vince opened his eyes and his angel was back. He sat up. He knew it was a dream and he was angry. "Are you back with more promises?" he asked the angel. "Save them, I can't afford it. The Lord came to my shop all right, and it cost me money," he added wondering where he got the courage to talk to an angel this way.

"Vince," the angel said gently. "The Lord has indeed visited your shop as I promised, but I believe that you missed him."

Vince interrupted, "Oh, I saw him all right, in 'the least of these.'"

The angel responded, "You're right. He is to be found in those such as the children and the homeless, but the Lord you missed was found elsewhere." The angel stopped and looked directly at Vince.

Vince was stumped. He tried to remember everyone who visited the shop since the angel's first visit. There was no one who qualified. Nothing special had happened.

"It was through you, Vince. The Lord came to the children when they received a fresh start with their balls. Your sleeper? He was fed freely and cared for. The Lord visited your shop through you, Vince." With that, Vince's angel was gone. He was wide awake, long before dawn. *"Was that a dream?"* he wondered. *"Was it a real angel?"* He picked up a shoe. A ball bounced down the staircase.

James Kasperson

From: *The Eternal Goodness*

I know not what the future hath
   Of marvel or surprise,
Assured alone that life and death
   His mercy underlies.

And if my heart and flesh are weak
   To bear an untried pain,
The bruised reed he will not break,
   But strengthen and sustain.

No offering of my own I have,
   Nor works my faith to prove;
I can but give the gifts he gave,
   And plead his love for love.

And so beside the silent sea
   I wait the muffled oar;
No harm from him can come to me
   On ocean or on shore.

I know not where his islands lift
   Their fronded palms in air;
I only know I cannot drift
   Beyond his love and care.

John Greenleaf Whittier
1807–1892

KENTUCKY WONDER

One of the greatest taste sensations from the home garden is freshly picked Kentucky Wonder pole beans. I remember savoring them as a child from my father's garden. And I now plant a few in my own garden patch each year.

In one recent summer, we had an incredibly difficult growing season in our area. Because of some extended weeks of drought, the rabbits and birds came after fresh bean sprouts not simply for food, but also for moisture. Only after three plantings and a careful fencing did my small crop of pole beans finally get established.

Early one July afternoon, I noticed some of the bean vines were headed off into emptiness. Instead of climbing the carefully placed poles, they were reaching out for some nonexistent support in the opposite direction. Carefully, and gently, I pulled the vine leaders from each misdirected plant toward the three poles, which formed a kind of tripod in the ground. I loosely wound each leader around one of the poles and hoped for the best.

Within hours, success was apparent. Each bean plant leader had quickly and tightly wrapped itself around the pole as though in reunion with a long-lost lover or family member. It was a marvelous phenomenon of nature to behold. Even after such a short time span, these plant leaders could not have been removed or changed from their new allegiance without seriously damaging the plant. They clutched the poles tenaciously.

How many persons around us are reaching out into emptiness these days, yearning for something solid upon which to cling? Do you know someone so disillusioned with the emptiness of life that he or she is reaching for something more substantial, enduring, or stable? Perhaps a neighbor? A family member? A friend? A co-worker?

Scores of people await only the caring, gentle assistance of a Christian friend to lead them to the firmly promised support of faith. Their longing may not be quite as apparent as those of my pole beans, but it is present and very intense. If such persons are simply encouraged, nudged, assisted, or invited in the direction of the authentic support of life, they will attach themselves and find their true home in due course.

Brian Kelley Bauknight

THE MUSTARD SEED

When they arrived at the bottom of the hill, a large crowd was waiting for them. A man came and knelt before Jesus and said, "Sir, have mercy on my son, for he is mentally deranged, and in great trouble, for he often falls into the fire or into the water; so I brought him to your disciples, but they couldn't cure him."

Jesus replied, "Oh, you stubborn, faithless people! How long shall I bear with you? Bring him here to me." Then Jesus rebuked the demon in the boy and it left him, and from that moment the boy was well.

Afterwards the disciples asked Jesus privately, "Why couldn't we cast that demon out?"

"Because of your little faith," Jesus told them. "For if you had faith even as small as a tiny mustard seed you could say to this mountain, 'Move!' and it would go far away. Nothing would be impossible."

Matthew 17:14-20 TLB

EVEN THE SMALLEST FAITH

God cautions us to be tender to His lambs, but no one can ever be as gentle as the Father Himself. Scripture lists three ranks of saints—"fathers," "young men," and "little children" (1 John 2:12-14). The Spirit of God shows His concern by mentioning the young ones first and delivering the sweet promise of mercy to them: "I write unto you, little children, for your sins are forgiven you for my name's sake" (v. 12). In plain terms He says their sins are forgiven. And at the same time He stops the mouth of guilt from discouraging them and opposing the Gospel—forgiven for His name's sake, a name far mightier than the name of a person's worst sin.

Sincerity, then, keeps up the soul's credit at the throne of grace so that no sin or weakness can hinder its welcome with God. Regarding iniquity in the heart, not just having it, keeps God from hearing our prayer (Psalm 66:18). This is a temptation which Christians often wrestle with when they let their personal shortcomings turn them away from prevailing prayer—they cower like some poor people who stay away from church because their clothing is not as fine as they would like.

To take care of this problem God has provided the promises—which, in any case, are our only ground for prayer—and has made them to fit the tiniest degree of grace. And as a well-done portrait faces everyone who enters the room, so the promises of the Gospel covenant smile upon everyone who sincerely looks to God in Christ. Scripture does not say, "If ye have faith like a cedar," but "if ye have faith as a grain of mustard seed" (Matthew 17:20). Justifying faith is not beneath miracle-working faith in its own sphere. The least sincere faith in Christ removes the mountainous guilt of sin from the soul. Thus every saint is said to have "like precious faith" (2 Peter 1:1). In Genesis we can barely see Sarah's faith, but in Hebrews 11 God gives it honorable mention, alongside Abraham's stronger faith.

William Gurnall

WHY FAITH IS COMPARED TO A SHIELD

The apostle compares faith to a shield because of a double resemblance between this grace and that particular piece of armor.

The first likeness is that the shield is not for the defense of any one part of the body, as most other pieces are. The helmet is fitted for the head and the plate designed for the breast, but the shield is intended for the defense of the whole body. Therefore it was to be made very large and was called a "gate" or "door" because it was so long and large that it covered the whole body. And if the shield was not large enough to cover every part at once, the skillful soldier could turn it this way or that way, to stop the swords or the arrows, no matter where they were directed. This resemblance reminds us of the importance of faith in the life of a Christian. It defends the whole man—every part of the Christian is preserved by it.

Sometimes the temptation is leveled at the head—at the saint's reasoning. Satan will dispute truth and, if he can, will make a Christian question the validity of faith merely because his understanding cannot comprehend it. And sometimes he prevails, blotting out a person's beliefs in the deity of Christ and in other great and profound truths of the Gospel. But faith intervenes between the believer and this arrow, coming to the relief of the Christian's weak understanding.

Abraham, "being not weak in faith . . . considered not his own body now dead" (Romans 4:19). If reason had had the upper hand in that business, if that holy man had put the promise to a test of sense and reason, he would have been in danger of questioning the truth of it, although God Himself was the messenger. But faith brought him through the test. "I will trust the Word of God," says the believer, "not my own blind reason."

William Gurnall

RIGHTEOUSNESS

"Blessed are they which do hunger and thirst after righteousness: for they shall be filled" (Matt. 5:6).

What a wonderful breadth of divine charity! He who is altogether righteous will accept from us even the thirst for righteousness. He will not reserve his blessing until I become actually pure, he will bless my very effort after purity. He will accept the mere desire of him; the mere wish of my heart to be like him; the mere throb of my pulse to be near him. Though I have not reached him, if only I see in him a beauty that I long for, he will count it unto me for righteousness. Though I claim not to be like him, and despair even to touch the hem of his garment, if only I can admire afar off the kingliness of his beauty, he will bless my very hunger and my very thirst for him.

Yet say not, Oh my soul, that thou hast salvation without goodness. Thou couldst not hunger after him, thou couldst not thirst for him, if he were not already in thee. . . . If thou were not like him, thou wouldst not see him as he is. If he were not in thee thou couldst not wish to imitate him—couldst not even feel the despair of imitating him.

Thou canst not admire what is out of thy nature, nor seek what is not kindred to thy being. . . . Thou canst cry out for outward food before thou knowest the taste thereof, but thou canst not cry for righteousness until thou has "tasted that the Lord is good." He who sees the King in his beauty has himself begun to be beautiful; he who hungers and thirsts after righteousness is already beginning to be filled.

George Matheson
1842–1906

THE MAID AWAKENED

(Matthew 9:18-26)

Once there was a girl twelve years of age who lived in a beautiful country house with her father and mother, who loved her dearly. Her father was one of the chief men of that place, a ruler, the president of Synagogue College, and very rich.

One day this little girl became ill, and day by day she grew weaker and weaker, until everybody feared she would never be well again. One morning she lay very white and still with her eyes closed and scarcely breathing. Her father had left his business that day to sit by her bedside and watch her. Tears filled his eyes as he thought he must lose his darling daughter. All at once the little girl opened her eyes and seeing her father's tears said: "Father, there's a good man who loves children. I saw him one day in town, and he looked at me and spoke to me so kindly, I just loved him. His name is Jesus. He heals the sick. I think he would make me well."

The father had thought of him several times, but as some of his friends didn't want to have anything to do with him, he did not go to him. But when his daughter whispered, "Please, father, tell him I'm sick," the father determined at once to go and get him. He hastened to the town where he was dining in a friend's house. He fell at the feet of the great Teacher, crying out: "My little daughter is dying! Please come quickly and lay your hand on the child, and she shall live!" At once the Teacher arose and followed the father, a great crowd of people following, each person trying to get near him and to look up into his face or to hear his wonderful words. As they were on their way a poor old woman that had been ill as many years as the little girl had been on the earth, with a disease that no doctor could cure, came up quietly behind Jesus in the crowd. She thought, "If I can only touch his garment, I shall be healed." And as soon as she put out her finger and touched the hem of his garment, she felt new life, and she was healed. "Who touched me?" said the great Teacher, turning around and looking straight at her. Then he spoke kind and comforting words to her. All this took so much time the father was worried and said, "O Sir, please hasten, or my little daughter will be dead before we get there!" But this great man was never in a hurry, having time to help everybody. They were not much farther on the way when they saw a man running toward them. It was the rich man's servant, who said, "Thy daughter is dead. Don't trouble the Teacher any further!" You should have seen the sorrow written on that poor father's face. Jesus saw it and said, "Do not be afraid. Only believe in me!" When they reached the house the doors were wide open and they heard the sound of pitiful wailing and weeping, accompanied by the flutes and other instruments of mourning-minstrels, who did not feel sad, but merely did this because they were paid for it. "Why make ye this ado and weep?" said Jesus. "The maid is not dead, but she is asleep!" After Jesus had passed, these weepers laughed and mocked him, saying, "We know she is dead."

"Come with me," said the Teacher with the gentle voice. Then he took the father and mother of the maid and three of his friends into the room where the maid was lying so white and still and breathless. Very tenderly he bent over her body, took her small white hand in his own warm hand, and softly said, "Little maid, arise!" In a moment the rose-color came back to her pale cheeks, and she sat up in the bed, and threw her arms about her father and mother, who could scarce believe their eyes for joy. Then she sprang from the bed and walked, perfectly well. "Give the maid something to eat," said the Teacher. Her mother quickly gave her something to eat. Soon the servants prepared a feast for the great Teacher, and the little maid sat next to him at the table, as happy and as well as she could be. And she never forgot the name of that great Friend who awakened her from her sleep of death!

William J. Sly

THE PRISONER AND
THE SHIPWRECK

(Acts 27)

"All aboard!" cried the captain of a sailing-vessel which was just loosing from the wharf to sail out to sea. There, on the deck, was a number of prisoners, guarded by soldiers. One of these prisoners was Paul, who had been seized in the temple at Jerusalem and nearly killed by a riotous mob. Forty men had secretly vowed not to eat or drink until they had killed him. The captain of the temple, being Paul's friend, told him about the plot, and sent him in the night with a guard of soldiers to the governor's house in a distant city. Paul said to the governor: "I want to have my case tried in Rome before the emperor, for I am a Roman citizen!" So Paul was sent as a prisoner to Rome on this sailing-vessel. Some of his friends were with him. One was "the beloved physician," Doctor Luke, who had often traveled with him on his missionary journeys and who is the man that tells this story. Out upon the great sea the ship sailed until it came to a wharf where there was a large wheat-ship sailing to Rome. Paul and the soldiers were put on board this wheat-ship. Counting the soldiers and passengers there were two hundred and seventy-six people in all. Soon their troubles began. The wind was blowing the wrong way, so that they had to go very slowly. But at last they came to Fair Havens, where they stayed much too long, Paul thought, for the stormy season of the year had come. Paul said, "You ought to stay here for the winter." But the captain of the soldiers only made fun of him. The weather just then seemed good, so they pulled up the anchors, hoisted the sails, and put out from Fair Havens. Hardly had they started when a terrible storm broke upon them, driving the ship far out of its course. The ship was in danger of breaking in two so that they had to throw great ropes around the ship to hold it together. Then they lowered the sails and let the vessel drift. For two weeks they were tossed and driven by the storm, not seeing the sun or stars. One night God sent to Paul an angel who said to him, "Fear not, Paul, you shall reach Rome in safety, and God will save all in the ship

with you." Early in the morning Paul said to the sailors and soldiers, "Be of good cheer, God will save you all." They made fun of
him, and the ship drifted on until in the darkness of the night they
found they were near some island. They quickly threw out four
anchors to save them from being dashed on the rocks, and longed
for the morning! As soon as daylight came and they saw the land,
some selfish sailors at the front of the boat pretending to put out
some more anchors, lowered the rowboat, and were just getting
ready to row away to the land, thinking only of saving themselves,
when Paul saw their trick and cried out to the soldiers, "Look!
except these men abide in the ship you yourselves cannot be
saved!" No one made fun of Paul then, but the soldiers ran and
cut away the rope of the boat and let the boat fall into the sea and
drift away. After they had eaten food they threw all their wheat
overboard to lighten the ship. As that did not help, they decided
to run the ship upon the shore, but the bow struck the beach and
the stern was broken to pieces by the fury of the waves. Some of
the soldiers said, "Kill all the prisoners, lest they swim to the shore
and escape." But the captain of the soldiers, who had grown to
think much of Paul, said: "No, but let each man who can swim
jump overboard and swim for the shore first." This they did, and
the others, including Paul and Doctor Luke, followed on planks
and other floating things from the ship. And all escaped safe to the
land. So Paul, the prisoner, was right; the ship was lost, but God
had saved all the two hundred and seventy-six men in the ship
with him!

William J. Sly

HOPE

Hope and faith are tied closely together. When we hope for something, we expect it to happen. We know that sometimes we must wait for it with patience. We believe God created us and the world, and that God plans good things for us. Sometimes disasters strike, but we can place our hopes in Jesus Christ and have faith that God's plan will always work in the end.

Christ is faithful as a son over God's house. And we are his house, if we hold on to our courage and the hope of which we boast.

Hebrews 3:6 NIV

EXPECT GOD'S BLESSINGS

Sincerity enables the Christian to think and speak well of God. A deceitful man's countenance droops and his heart enlarges with venom against God. He dares not let it come out of his mouth but it festers in his deepest thoughts. Because the wretched man does not love God, he has no place in his soul to reflect on God's goodness. He fumes and frets and forgets the abundant blessings God has brought in the past and gives in to resentment because of his present problems. And he would much rather curse God than take the blame himself.

But the sincere Christian cherishes such sweet thoughts of God that his meditations unite him with peace and he would not consider speaking unworthily of God's glory or goodness. We see this in David: "I was dumb, I opened not my mouth; because thou didst it" (Psalm 39:9). Both his spirit and body were afflicted at the same time; he was sad and sick, yet he remembered where the affliction came from. "This is from You, Lord, and I love You dearly; so I can take it without fear. After all, You might have thrown me into a bed of flames instead of a bed of sickness; so let me accept my correction thankfully." Thus he fielded the blow without sending words of resentment or anger back upon God.

Sincerity enables the soul to expect good from God. It would break a heart of stone to read the sad cries which David's soul made when he was in anguish of flesh and agony of spirit. Yet even in this storm he cast out his anchor until it took hold of God: "In thee, O Lord, do I hope: thou wilt hear, O Lord my God" (Psalm 38:15). His expectation of good from God absorbed the bitterness coming from his pain: "I am poor and needy; yet the Lord thinketh upon me" (Psalm 40:17). His condition was pitiful but his comfort was even stronger: "God has not thrown me away. I am in His mind day and night, and His thoughts are at work to do me good."

William Gurnall

Hope in the Darkness

Say not the struggle naught availeth,
   The labour and the wounds are vain,
The enemy faints not, nor faileth,
   And as things have been they remain.

If hopes were dupes, fears may be liars;
   It may be, in yon smoke concealed,
Your comrades chase e'en now the fliers,
   And, but for you, possess the field.

For while the tired waves, vainly breaking,
   Seem here no painful inch to gain,
Far back, through creeks and inlets making,
   Comes silent, flooding in, the main.

And not by eastern windows only,
   When daylight comes, comes in the light;
In front the sun climbs slow, how slowly!
   But westward, look, the land is bright!

Arthur Hugh Clough
1819–1861

HOPE AND WORTHY ACHIEVEMENTS

Hope of salvation moves the Christian to perform high and worthy services. It is a grace conceived for great action. As carnal hope stirs carnal men to achievements which gain them a reputation in the world, so this heavenly hope influences the saint's undertakings.

What makes the daring soldier rush into the mouth of death itself? He hopes to rescue honor from the jaws of death. Hope is the helmet and shield which make him calm in the face of every danger. What makes a man tear his hands and crawl up some craggy mountain which proves only a bleak, barren place to stand in? There he is wrapped up in clouds and can look over other men's heads and see a little farther than they. Now if these hopes—which borrow motives from human ambition and imagination—turn men toward accomplishments, how much more does the believer's hope of eternal life provoke him to noble exploits! Let us look at some examples.

Hope frees from lust. When Moses came to give Israel the hope of God's approaching salvation, his people experienced a mighty change. Whereas they had cowered under Egyptian burdens and had not tried to shake off the oppressor's yoke, now they broke free and marched toward their promised rest. It did not seem to make any difference that Pharaoh chased them with a raging determination—they were fortified with hope.

How helpless is the person who does not have this heavenly hope! Satan makes a slave of him and he becomes the footstool for the every base lust to trample upon. He lets the devil ride him anywhere, at any time. No mud puddle is too filthy for Satan to lead him through with a twine thread. And the poor man follows because he does not know a better master, nor better wages than the sensual pleasures of his lusts.

William Gurnall

PATIENCE

Blessed be the God and Father of our Lord Jesus Christ! By his great mercy he has given us a new birth into a living hope through the resurrection of Jesus Christ from the dead, and into an inheritance that is imperishable, undefiled, and unfading, kept in heaven for you, who are being protected by the power of God through faith for a salvation ready to be revealed in the last time. In this you rejoice, even if now for a little while you have had to suffer various trials, so that the genuineness of your faith — being more precious than gold that, though perishable is tested by fire — may be found to result in praise and glory and honor when Jesus Christ is revealed. Although you have not seen him, you love him; and even though you do not see him now, you believe in him and rejoice with an indescribable and glorious joy, for you are receiving the outcome of our faith, the salvation of your souls.

If you endure when you are beaten for doing wrong, what credit is that? But if you endure when you do right and suffer for it, you have God's approval. For to this you have been called, because Christ also suffered for you, leaving you an example, so that you should follow in his steps.

"He committed no sin, and no
deceit was found in his mouth."

When he was abused, he did not return abuse; when he suffered, he did not threaten; but he entrusted himself to the one who judges justly. He himself bore our sins in his body on the cross, so that, free from sins, we might live for righteousness; by his wounds you have been healed. For you were going astray like sheep, but now you have returned to the shepherd and guardian of your souls.

1 Peter 1:3-9; 2:20-25 NRSV

A FAR, FAR BETTER THING

They said of him, about the city that night, that it was the peacefullest man's face ever beheld there. Many added that he looked sublime and prophetic.

One of the most remarkable sufferers by the same axe—a woman—had asked at the foot of the same scaffold, not long before, to be allowed to write down the thoughts that were inspiring her. If he had given any utterance to his, and they were prophetic, they would have been these:

"I see a beautiful city and a brilliant people rising from this abyss, and, in their struggles to be truly free, in their triumphs and defeats, through long years to come, I see the evil of this time and of the previous time of which this is the natural birth, gradually making expiation for itself and wearing out.

"I see the lives for which I lay down my life, peaceful, useful, prosperous and happy, in that England which I shall see no more. I see her with a child upon her bosom, who bears my name. I see her father, aged and bent, but otherwise restored, and faithful to all men in his healing office, and at peace. . . .

"I see that I hold a sanctuary in their hearts, and in the hearts of their descendants, generations hence. . . .

"I see that child who lay upon her bosom and who bore my name, a man winning his way up in that path of life which once was mine. I see him winning it so well, that my name is made illustrious there by the light of his. I see the blots I threw upon it, faded away. I see him, foremost of just judges and honoured men, bringing a boy of my name, with a forehead that I know and golden hair, to this place, then fair to look upon, with not a trace of this day's disfigurement—and I hear him tell the child my story, with a tender and faltering voice.

"It is a far, far better thing that I do, than I have ever done; it is a far, far better rest that I go to, than I have ever known."

Charles Dickens, in
A Tale of Two Cities

REJOICE IN HOPE

Waiting on God for deliverance during affliction is closely linked with holy silence. "Truly my soul waiteth upon God: from him cometh my salvation" (Psalm 62:1). The Hebrew literally reads, "My soul is silent."

Hope fills the afflicted soul with joy. Hope brings such consolation that the afflicted soul can smile even when tears run down the face. This is called "the rejoicing of the hope" (Hebrews 3:6). And hope never produces more joy than in affliction. The sun paints the beautiful colors in the rainbow on a watery cloud. "Rejoice in hope of the glory of God. And not only so, but we glory in tribulations" (Romans 5:2-3). Glorying is a rejoicing which the Christian cannot contain within himself; it comes forth in some outward expression to let others know what a feast he has inside. The springs of comfort lie high indeed when joy flows from the believer's mouth. And all the joy which sustains the suffering saint is sent in by hope at the cost of Christ, who has prepared unspeakable glory in heaven. Should we pity ourselves for the tribulations we go through on the way to Christ's glory?

While troubles attack with oppression, the gracious promises anoint with blessings. Hope breaks the alabaster box of the promises over the Christian's head and sends consolations abroad in the soul. And like a precious ointment these comforts exhilarate and refresh the spirit, heal the wounds, and remove the pain. Paul says, "Hope maketh not ashamed; because the love of God is shed abroad in our hearts by the Holy Ghost which is given unto us" (Romans 5:5).

Faith and hope are two graces which Christ uses above all others to fill the soul with joy, because these fetch all their wine of joy out of doors. Faith tells the soul what Christ has done and hope revives the soul with the news of what He will do. But both draw sweet wine from the same source—Christ and His promise.

William Gurnall

Dominus Illuminatio Mea

In the hour of death, after this life's whim,
When the heart beats low, and the eyes grow dim,
And pain has exhausted every limb —
    The lover of the Lord shall trust in him.

When the will has forgotten the lifelong aim,
And the mind can only disgrace its fame,
And a man is uncertain of his own name —
    The power of the Lord shall fill this frame.

When the last sigh is heaved, and the last tear shed,
And the coffin is waiting beside the bed,
And the widow and child forsake the dead —
    The angel of the Lord shall lift this head.

For even the purest delight may pall,
And power must fail, and the pride must fall,
And the love of the dearest friends grow small —
    But the glory of the Lord is all in all.

Richard Doddridge Blackmore
1825–1900

THE MASTER OF THE HARVEST

The Master of the Harvest walked by the side of his cornfields in the springtime. A frown was on his face, for there had been no rain for several weeks, and the earth was hard from the parching of the east winds. The young wheat had not been able to spring up.

So as he looked over the long ridges that stretched in rows before him, he was vexed and began to grumble and say:—

"The harvest will be backward, and all things will go wrong."

Then he frowned more and more, and uttered complaints against Heaven because there was no rain; against the earth because it was so dry; against the corn because it had not sprung up.

And the Master's discontent was whispered all over the field, and along the ridges where the corn-seed lay. And the poor little seeds murmured:—

"How cruel to complain! Are we not doing our best? Have we let one drop of moisture pass by unused? Are we not striving every day to be ready for the hour of breaking forth? Are we idle? How cruel to complain!"

But of all this the Master of the Harvest heard nothing, so the gloom did not pass from his face. Going to his comfortable home he repeated to his wife the dark words, that the drought would ruin the harvest, for the corn was not yet sprung up.

Then his wife spoke cheering words, and taking her Bible she wrote some texts upon the flyleaf, and after them the date of the day.

And the words she wrote were these: "The eyes of all wait upon Thee; and Thou givest them their meat in due season. Thou openest Thine hand and satisfiest the desire of every living thing. How excellent is Thy loving-kindness, O God! therefore the children of men put their trust under the shadow of Thy wings. Thou hast put gladness in my heart, more than in the time that their corn and their wine increased" (Psalm 36:7-9 KJV).

And so a few days passed as before, and the house was gloomy with the discontent of the Master. But at last one evening there was rain all over the land, and when the Master of the Harvest went out the next morning for his early walk by the cornfields, the corn had sprung up at last.

The young shoots burst out at once, and very soon all along the ridges were to be seen rows of tender blades, tinting the whole field with a delicate green. And day by day the Master of the Harvest saw them, and was satisfied, but he spoke of other things and forgot to rejoice.

Then a murmur rose among the corn-blades. "The Master was angry because we did not come up; now that we have come forth why is he not glad? Are we not doing our best? From morning and evening dews, from the glow of the sun, from the juices of the earth, from the freshening breezes, even from clouds and rain, are we not taking food and strength, warmth and life? Why does he not rejoice?"

And when the Master's wife asked him if the wheat was doing well he answered, "Fairly well," and nothing more.

But the wife opened her Book, and wrote again on the flyleaf: "Who hath divided a watercourse for the overflowing of waters, or a way for the lightning of thunder, to cause it to rain on the earth where no man is, on the wilderness wherein there is no man, to satisfy the desolate and waste ground, and to cause the bud of the tender herb to spring forth? For He maketh small the drops of water; they pour down rain according to the vapor thereof, which the clouds do drop and distil upon man abundantly. Also can any understand the spreadings of the clouds, or the noise of his tabernacle?" (Job 38:25-27; 36:29 KJV).

Very peaceful were the next few weeks. All nature seemed to rejoice in the fine weather. The corn-blades shot up strong and tall. They burst into flowers and gradually ripened into ears of grain. But alas! The Master of the Harvest had still some fault to find. He looked at the ears and saw that they were small. He grumbled and said:—

"The yield will be less than it ought to be. The harvest will be bad."

And the voice of his discontent was breathed over the cornfield where the plants were growing and growing. They shuddered and murmured: "How thankless to complain! Are we not growing as fast as we can? If we were idle would we bear wheat-ears at all? How thankless to complain!"

Meanwhile a few weeks went by and a drought settled on the land. Rain was needed, so that the corn-ears might fill. And behold, while the wish for rain was yet on the Master's lips, the sky became full of heavy clouds, darkness spread over the land, a wild wind arose, and the roaring of thunder announced a storm. And such a storm! Along the ridges of corn-plants drove the rain-laden wind, and the plants bent down before it and rose again like the waves of the sea. They bowed down and they rose up. Only where the whirlwind was the strongest they fell to the ground and could not rise again.

And when the storm was over, the Master of the Harvest saw here and there patches of over-weighted corn, yet dripping from the thundershower, and he grew angry with them, and forgot to think of the long ridges where the corn-plants were still standing tall and strong, and where the corn-ears were swelling and rejoicing.

His face grew darker than ever. He railed against the rain. He railed against the sun because it did not shine. He blamed the wheat because it might perish before the harvest.

"But why does he always complain?" moaned the corn-plants. "Have we not done our best from the first? Has not God's blessing been with us? Are we not growing daily more beautiful in strength and hope? Why does not the Master trust, as we do, in the future richness of the harvest?"

Of all this the Master of the Harvest heard nothing. But his wife wrote on the flyleaf of her Book: "He watereth the hills from his chambers, the earth is satisfied with the fruit of thy works. He causeth the grass to grow for the cattle and herb for the service of man, that he may bring forth food out of the earth, and wine that maketh glad the heart of man, and oil to make his face to shine, and bread which strengtheneth man's heart" (Psalm 104:13-15 KJV).

And day by day the hours of sunshine were more in number. And by degrees the green corn-ears ripened into yellow, and the yellow turned into gold, and the abundant harvest was ready, and the laborers were not wanting.

Then the bursting corn broke out into songs of rejoicing. "At least we have not labored and watched in vain! Surely the earth hath yielded her increase! Blessed be the Lord who daily loadeth us with benefits! Where now is the Master of the Harvest? Come, let him rejoice with us!"

And the Master's wife brought out her Book and her husband read the texts she had written even from the day when the corn-seeds were held back by the first drought, and as he read a new heart seemed to grow within him, a heart that was thankful to the Lord of the Great Harvest. And he read aloud from the Book:—

"Thou visitest the earth and waterest it; thou greatly enrichest it with the river of God which is full of water; thou preparest them corn, when thou hast so provided for it. Thou waterest the ridges thereof abundantly; thou settlest the furrows thereof; thou makest it soft with showers; thou blessest the springing thereof. Thou crownest the year with thy goodness, and thy paths drop fatness. They drop upon the pastures of the wilderness, and the little hills rejoice on every side. The pastures are clothed with flocks. The valleys also are covered over with corn; they shout for joy, they also sing.—O that men would praise the Lord for His goodness, and for his wonderful works to the children of men!" (Psalm 65:9-13).

Mrs. Alfred Gatty (ADAPTED)

THE GREAT STONE FACE

The Great Stone Face was a work of Nature in her mood of majestic playfulness, formed on the perpendicular side of a mountain by some immense rocks, which had been thrown together in such a position as, when viewed at a proper distance, precisely to resemble the features of the human countenance. It seemed as if an enormous giant, or a Titan, had sculptured his own likeness on the precipice. There was the broad arch of the forehead, a hundred feet in height; the nose, with its long bridge; and the vast lips, which, if they could have spoken, would have rolled their thunder accents from one end of the valley to the other. The Great Stone Face seemed positively to be alive.

It was a happy lot for children to grow up to manhood or womanhood with the Great Stone Face before their eyes, for all the features were noble, and the expression was at once grand and sweet, as if it were the glow of a vast, warm heart, that embraced all mankind in its affections, and had room for more. It was an education only to look at it. According to the belief of many people, the valley owed much of its fertility to this benign aspect that was continually beaming over it, illuminating the clouds, and infusing its tenderness into the sunshine.

A mother and her little boy sat at their cottage-door, gazing at the Great Stone Face, and talking about it. The child's name was Ernest.

"Mother," said he, while the Titanic visage smiled on him, "I wish that it could speak, for it looks so very kindly that its voice must needs be pleasant. If I were to see a man with such a face, I should love him dearly."

"If an old prophecy should come to pass," answered his mother, "we may see a man, some time or other, with exactly such a face as that."

"What prophecy do you mean, dear mother?" eagerly inquired Ernest. "Pray tell me all about it!"

So his mother told him a story that her own mother had told to her, when she herself was younger than little Ernest; a story, not of things that were past, but of what was yet to come; a story, nevertheless, so very old, that even the Indians, who formerly inhabited this valley, had heard it from their forefathers, to whom, as they affirmed, it had been murmured by the mountain streams, and whispered by the wind among the tree-tops. The purport was, that, at some future day, a child should be born hereabouts, who was destined to become the greatest and noblest personage of his time, and whose countenance, in manhood, should bear an exact resemblance to the Great Stone Face.

"O mother, dear mother!" cried Ernest, clapping his hands above his head, "I do hope that I shall live to see him!"

And Ernest never forgot the story that his mother told him. He spent his childhood in the log-cottage where he was born, and was dutiful to his mother, and helpful to her in many things, assisting her much with his little hands, and more with his loving heart. In this manner, from a happy yet often pensive child, he grew up to be a mild, quiet, unobtrusive boy, and sun-browned with labor in the fields, but with more intelligence brightening his aspect than is seen in many lads who have been taught at famous schools. Yet Ernest had had no teacher, save only that the Great Stone Face became one to him. When the toil of the day was over, he would gaze at it for hours, until he began to imagine that those vast features recognized him, and gave him a smile of kindness and encouragement, responsive to his own look of veneration. We must not take upon us to affirm that this was a mistake, although the Face may have looked no more kindly at Ernest than at all the world besides. But the secret was that the boy's tender and confiding simplicity discerned what other people could not see; and thus the love, which was meant for all, became his peculiar portion.

About this time there went a rumor throughout the valley, that the great man, foretold from ages long ago, who was to bear a resemblance to the Great Stone Face, had appeared at last. It seems that, many years before, a young man had migrated from the valley and settled at a distant seaport, where, after getting together a little money, he had set up as a shopkeeper. His name — but I could never learn whether it was his real one, or a nickname that had grown out of his habits and success in life — was Gathergold. Being shrewd and active, and endowed by Providence with that inscrutable faculty which develops itself in what the world calls luck, he became an exceedingly rich merchant, and owner of a whole fleet of bulky-bottomed ships. All the countries of the globe appeared to join hands for the mere purpose of adding heap after heap to the mountainous accumulation of this one man's wealth. The cold regions of the North, almost within the gloom and shadow of the Arctic Circle, sent him their tribute in the shape of furs; hot Africa sifted for him the golden sands of her rivers, and gathered up the ivory tusks of her great elephants out of the forests; the East came bringing him the rich shawls, and spices, and teas, and the effulgence of diamonds, and the gleaming purity of large pearls. The ocean, not to be behindhand with the earth, yielded up her mighty whales, that Mr. Gathergold might sell their oil, and make a profit on it. Be the original commodity what it might, it was gold within his grasp. And, when Mr. Gathergold had become so very rich that it would have taken him a hundred years only to count his wealth, he bethought himself of his native valley, and resolved to go back thither, and end his days where he was born. With this purpose in view, he sent a skillful architect to build him such a palace as should be fit for a man of his vast wealth to live in.

As I have said above, it had already been rumored in the valley that Mr. Gathergold had turned out to be the prophetic personage so long and vainly looked for, and that his visage was the perfect and undeniable similitude of the Great Stone Face. People were the more ready to believe that this must needs be the fact, when they beheld the splendid edifice that rose, as if by enchantment, on the site of his father's old weather-beaten farm-house. Mr. Gathergold's bedchamber, especially, made such a glittering appearance that no ordinary man would have been able to close his eyes there. But, on the other hand, Mr. Gathergold was now so inured to wealth, that perhaps he could not have closed his eyes unless where the gleam of it was certain to find its way beneath his eyelids.

In due time, the mansion was finished; next came the upholsterers, with magnificent furniture; then, a whole troop of black and white servants, the harbingers of Mr. Gathergold, who, in his own majestic person, was expected to arrive at sunset. Our friend Ernest, meanwhile, had been deeply stirred by the idea that the great man, the noble man, the man of prophecy, after so many ages of delay, was at length to be made manifest to his native valley. He knew, boy as he was, that there were a thousand ways in which Mr. Gathergold, with his vast wealth, might transform himself into an angel of beneficence, and assume a control over human affairs as wide and benignant as the smile of the Great Stone Face. Full of faith and hope, Ernest doubted not that what the people said was true, and that now he was to behold the living likeness of those wondrous features on the mountain-side. While the boy was still gazing up the valley, and fancying, as he always did, that the Great Stone Face returned his gaze and looked kindly at him, the rumbling of wheels was heard, approaching swiftly along the winding road.

A carriage, drawn by four horses, dashed round the turn of the road. Within it, thrust partly out of the window, appeared the physiognomy of the old man, with a skin as yellow as if his own Midas-hand had transmuted it. He had a low forehead, small, sharp eyes, puckered about with innumerable wrinkles, and very thin lips, which he made still thinner by pressing them forcibly together.

"The very image of the Great Stone Face!" shouted the people. "Sure enough, the old prophecy is true; and here we have the great man come, at last!"

And, what greatly perplexed Ernest, they seemed actually to believe that here was the likeness which they spoke of. By the roadside there chanced to be an old beggar-woman and two little beggar-children, stragglers from some far-off region, who, as the carriage rolled onward, held out their hands and lifted up their doleful voices, most piteously beseeching charity. A yellow claw—the very same that had clawed together so much wealth—poked itself out of the coach-window, and dropped some copper coins upon the ground; so that, though the great man's name seems to have been Gathergold, he might just as suitably have been nicknamed Scattercopper. Still, nevertheless, with an earnest shout, and evidently with as much good faith as ever, the people bellowed:

"He is the very image of the Great Stone Face!"

But Ernest turned sadly from the wrinkled shrewdness of that sordid visage, and gazed up the valley, where, amid a gathering mist, gilded by the last sunbeams, he could still distinguish those glorious features which had impressed themselves into his soul. Their aspect cheered him. What did the benign lips seem to say?

"He will come! Fear not, Ernest; the man will come!"

The years went on, and Ernest ceased to be a boy. He had grown to be a young man now. He attracted little notice from the other inhabitants of the valley; for they saw nothing remarkable in his way of life, save that, when the labor of the day was over, he still loved to go apart and gaze and meditate upon the Great Stone Face. According to their idea of the matter, it was a folly, indeed, but pardonable, inasmuch as Ernest was industrious, kind, and neighborly, and neglected no duty for the sake of indulging this idle habit. A simple soul, — simple as when his mother first taught him the old prophecy, — he beheld the marvelous features beaming adown the valley, and still wondered that their human counterpart was so long in making his appearance.

By this time poor Mr. Gathergold was dead and buried; and the oddest part of the matter was, that his wealth, which was the body and spirit of his existence, had disappeared before his death, leaving nothing of him but a living skeleton, covered over with a wrinkled, yellow skin. Since the melting away of his gold, it had been very generally conceded that there was no such striking resemblance, after all, betwixt the ignoble features of the ruined merchant and that majestic face upon the mountain-side. So the people ceased to honor him during his lifetime, and quietly consigned him to forgetfulness after his decease.

It so happened that a native-born son of the valley, many years before, had enlisted as a soldier, and, after a great deal of hard fighting, had now become an illustrious commander. Whatever he may be called in history, he was known in camps and on the battle-field under the nickname of Old Blood-and-Thunder. This war-worn veteran, being now infirm with age and wounds, and weary of the turmoil of a military life, and of the roll of the drum and the clangor of the trumpet, that had so long been ringing in his ears, had lately signified a purpose of returning to his native valley, hoping to find repose where he remembered to have left it. The inhabitants, his old neighbors and their grown-up children, were resolved to welcome the renowned warrior with a salute of cannon and a public dinner; and all the more enthusiastically, it being affirmed that now, at last, the likeness of the Great Stone Face had actually appeared. Great, therefore, was the excitement throughout the valley; and many people, who had never once thought of glancing at the Great Stone Face for years before, now spent their time in gazing at it, for the sake of knowing exactly how General Blood-and-Thunder looked.

On the day of the great festival, Ernest, with all the other people of the valley, left their work, and proceeded to the spot where the sylvan banquet was prepared. As he approached, the loud voice of the Rev. Dr. Battleblast was heard, beseeching a blessing on the good things set before them, and on the distinguished friend of peace in whose honor they were assembled. The tables were arranged in a cleared space of the woods, shut in by the surrounding trees, except where a vista opened eastward, and afforded a distant view of the Great Stone Face. Our friend Ernest raised himself on his tiptoes, in hopes to get a glimpse of the celebrated guest; but there was a mighty crowd about the tables anxious to hear the toasts and speeches, and to catch any word that might fall from the general in reply; and a volunteer company, doing duty as a guard, pricked ruthlessly with their bayonets at any particularly quiet person among the throng. So Ernest, being of an unobtrusive character, was thrust quite into the background, where he could see no more of Old Blood-and-Thunder's physiognomy than if it had been still blazing on the battle-field. To console himself, he turned towards the Great Stone Face, which, like a faithful and long-remembered friend, looked back and smiled upon him through the vista of the forest. Meantime, however, he could overhear the remarks of various individuals, who were comparing the features of the hero with the face on the distant mountain-side.

" 'T is the same face, to a hair!" cried one man, cutting a caper for joy.

"Wonderfully like, that's a fact!" responded another.

All these comments, and this vast enthusiasm, served the more to interest our friend; nor did he think of questioning that now, at length, the mountain-visage had found its human counterpart. It is true, Ernest had imagined that this long-looked-for personage would appear in the character of a man of peace, uttering wisdom, and doing good, and making people happy. But, taking an habitual breadth of view, with all his simplicity, he contended that Providence should choose its own method of blessing mankind, and could conceive that this great end might be effected even by a warrior and a bloody sword, should inscrutable wisdom see fit to order matters so.

"The general! the general!" was now the cry. "Hush! silence! Old Blood-and-Thunder's going to make a speech."

Even so; for, the cloth being removed, the general's health had been drunk, amid shouts of applause, and he now stood upon his feet to thank the company. Ernest saw him. And there, too, visible in the same glance, through the vista of the forest, appeared the Great Stone Face! And was there, indeed, such a resemblance as the crowd had testified? Alas, Ernest could not recognize it! He beheld a war-worn and weather-beaten countenance, full of energy, and expressive of an iron will; but the gentle wisdom, the deep, broad, tender sympathies, were altogether wanting in Old Blood-and-Thunder's visage; and even if the Great Stone Face had assumed his look of stern command, the milder traits would still have tempered it.

"This is not the man of prophecy," sighed Ernest to himself, as he made his way out of the throng. "And must the world wait longer yet?"

The mists had congregated about the distant mountain-side, and there were seen the grand and awful features of the Great Stone Face, awful but benignant, as if a mighty angel were sitting among the hills, and enrobing himself in a cloud-vesture of gold and purple. As he looked, Ernest could hardly believe but that a smile beamed over the whole visage, with a radiance still brightening, although without motion of the lips. It was probably the effect of the western sunshine, melting through the thinly diffused vapors that had swept between him and the object that he gazed at. But—as it always did—the aspect of his marvelous friend made Ernest as hopeful as if he had never hoped in vain.

"Fear not, Ernest," said his heart, even as if the Great Face were whispering to him,—"fear not, Ernest; he will come."

More years sped swiftly and tranquilly away. Ernest still dwelt in his native valley, and was now a man of middle age. By imperceptible degrees, he had become known among the people. Now, as heretofore, he labored for his bread, and was the same simple-hearted man that he had always been. But he had thought and felt so much, he had given so many of the best hours of his life to unworldly hopes for some great good to mankind, that it seemed as though he had been talking with the angels, and had imbibed a portion of their wisdom unawares. It was visible in the calm and well-considered beneficence of his daily life, the quiet stream of which had made a wide green margin all along its course. Not a day passed by, that the world was not the better because this man, humble as he was, had lived. He never stepped aside from his own path, yet would always reach a blessing to his neighbor. Almost involuntarily, too, he had become a preacher. The pure and high simplicity of his thought, which, as one of its manifestations, took shape in the good deeds that dropped silently from his hand, flowed also forth in speech. He uttered truths that wrought upon and molded the lives of those who heard him. His auditors, it may be, never suspected that Ernest, their own neighbor and familiar friend, was more than an ordinary man; least of all did Ernest himself suspect it; but, inevitably as the murmur of a rivulet, came thoughts out of his mouth that no other human lips had spoken.

When the people's minds had had a little time to cool, they were ready enough to acknowledge their mistake in imagining a similarity between General Blood-and-Thunder's truculent physiognomy and the benign visage on the mountain-side. But now, again, there were reports and many paragraphs in the newspapers, affirming that the likeness of the Great Stone Face had appeared upon the broad shoulders of a certain eminent statesman. He, like Mr. Gathergold and Old Blood-and-Thunder, was a native of the valley, but had left it in his early days, and taken up the trades of law and politics. Instead of the rich man's wealth and the warrior's sword, he had but a tongue, and it was mightier than both together. So wonderfully eloquent was he, that whatever he might choose to say, his auditors had no choice but to believe him; wrong looked like right, and right like wrong; for when it pleased him, he could make a kind of illuminated fog with his mere breath, and obscure the natural daylight with it. His tongue, indeed, was a magic instrument: sometimes it rumbled like the thunder; sometimes it warbled like the sweetest music. It was the blast of war, — the song of peace; and it seemed to have a heart in it, when there was no such matter. In good truth, he was a wondrous man; and when his tongue had acquired him all other imaginable success, — when it had been heard in halls of state, and in the courts of princes and potentates, — after it had made him known all over the world, even as a voice crying from shore to shore, — it finally persuaded his countrymen to select him for the Presidency. Before this time, — indeed, as soon as he began to grow celebrated, — his admirers had found out the resemblance between him and the Great Stone Face; and so much were they struck by it, that throughout the country this distinguished gentleman was known by the name of Old Stony Phiz.

While this friends were doing their best to make him President, Old Stony Phiz, as he was called, set out on a visit to the valley where he was born. Of course, he had no other object than to shake hands with his fellow-citizens, and neither thought nor cared about any effect which his progress through the country might have upon the election. Magnificent preparations were made to receive the illustrious statesman; a cavalcade of horsemen set forth to meet him at the boundary line of the State, and all the people left their business and gathered along the wayside to see him pass. Among these was Ernest. Though more than once disappointed, as we have seen, he had such a hopeful and confiding nature, that he was always ready to believe in whatever seemed beautiful and good.

The cavalcade came prancing along the road, with a great clattering of hoofs and a mighty cloud of dust, which rose up so dense and high that the visage of the mountain-side was completely hid-

den from Ernest's eyes. All the great men of the neighborhood
were there on horseback; militia officers, in uniform; the member
of Congress; the sheriff of the county; the editors of newspapers,
and many a farmer, too, had mounted his patient steed, with his
Sunday coat upon his back. It really was a very brilliant spectacle,
especially as there were numerous banners flaunting over the cavalcade, on some of which were gorgeous portraits of the illustrious
statesman and the Great Stone Face, smiling familiarly at one
another, like two brothers. If the pictures were to be trusted, the
mutual resemblance, it must be confessed was marvelous.

All this while the people were throwing up their hats and shouting, with enthusiasm so contagious that the heart of Ernest kin-
dled up, and he likewise threw up his hat, and shouted, as loudly
as the loudest, "Huzza for the great man! Huzza for Old Stony
Phiz!" But as yet he had not seen him.

In the midst of all this gallant array came an open barouche,
drawn by four white horses; and in the barouche, with his massive
head uncovered, sat the illustrious statesman, Old Stony Phiz
himself.

"Confess it," said one of Ernest's neighbors to him, "the Great
Stone Face has met its match at last!"

Now, it must be owned that, at his first glimpse of the countenance which was bowing and smiling from the barouche, Ernest
did fancy that there was a resemblance between it and the old
familiar face upon the mountain-side. The brow, with its massive
depth and loftiness, and all the other features, indeed, were bold-
ly and strongly hewn, as if in emulation of a more than heroic, of
a Titanic model. But the sublimity and stateliness, the grand
expression of a divine sympathy, that illuminated the mountain
visage and etherealized its ponderous granite substance into spirit, might here be sought in vain. Something had been originally
left out, or had departed. And therefore the marvelously gifted
statesman had always a weary gloom in the deep caverns of his
eyes, as of a child that has outgrown its playthings or a man of
mighty faculties and little aims, whose life, with all its high per-
formances, was vague and empty, because no high purpose had
endowed it with reality.

Still, Ernest's neighbor was thrusting his elbow into his side, and pressing him for an answer.

"Confess! confess! Is not he the very picture of your Old Man of the Mountain?"

"No!" said Ernest, bluntly, "I see little or no likeness."

"Then so much the worse for the Great Stone Face!" answered his neighbor; and again he set up a shout for Old Stony Phiz.

But Ernest turned away, melancholy, and almost despondent: for this was the saddest of his disappointments, to behold a man who might have fulfilled the prophecy, and had not willed to do so. Meantime, the cavalcade, the banners, the music, and the barouches swept past him, and the vociferous crowd in the rear, leaving the dust to settle down, and the Great Stone Face to be revealed again, with the grandeur that it had worn for untold centuries.

"Lo, here I am, Ernest!" the benign lips seemed to say. "I have waited longer than thou, and am not yet weary. Fear not; the man will come."

The years hurried onward, treading in their haste on one another's heels. And now they began to bring white hairs, and scatter them over the head of Ernest; they made reverend wrinkles across his forehead, and furrows in his cheeks. He was an aged man. But not in vain had he grown old: more than the white hairs on his head were the sage thoughts in his mind; his wrinkles and furrows were inscriptions that Time had graved, and in which he had written legends of wisdom that had been tested by the tenor of a life. And Ernest had ceased to be obscure. Unsought for, undesired, had come the fame which so many seek, and made him known in the great world, beyond the limits of the valley in which he had dwelt so quietly. College professors, and even the active men of cities, came from far to see and converse with Ernest; for the report had gone abroad that this simple husbandman had ideas unlike those of other men, not gained from books, but of a higher tone,—a tranquil and familiar majesty, as if he had been talking with the angels as his daily friends. Whether it were sage, statesman, or philanthropist, Ernest received these visitors with the gentle sincerity that had characterized him from boyhood, and spoke freely with them of whatever came uppermost, or lay deepest in his heart or their own. While they talked together, his face would kindle, unawares, and shine upon them, as with a mild evening light. Pensive with the fulness of such discourse, his guests took leave and went their way; and passing up the valley, paused to look at the Great Stone Face, imagining that they had seen its likeness in a human countenance, but could not remember where.

While Ernest had been growing up and growing old, a bountiful Providence had granted a new poet to this earth. He, likewise, was a native of the valley, but had spent the greater part of his life at a distance from that romantic region, pouring out his sweet music amid the bustle and din of cities. Often, however, did the mountains which had been familiar to him in his childhood lift their snowy peaks into the clear atmosphere of his poetry. Neither was the Great Stone Face forgotten, for the poet had celebrated it in an ode, which was grand enough to have been uttered by its own majestic lips. This man of genius, we may say, had come down from heaven with wonderful endowments. The world assumed another and a better aspect from the hour that the poet blessed it with his happy eyes. The Creator had bestowed him, as the last best touch to his own handiwork. Creation was not finished till the poet came to interpret, and so complete it.

The effect was no less high and beautiful, when his human brethren were the subject of his verse. He showed the golden links of the great chain that intertwined them with an angelic kindred; he brought out the hidden traits of a celestial birth that made them worthy of such kin.

The songs of this poet found their way to Ernest. He read them after his customary toil, seated on the bench before his cottage-door, where for such a length of time he had filled his repose with thought, by gazing at the Great Stone Face. And now as he read stanzas that caused the soul to thrill within him, he lifted his eyes to the vast countenance beaming on him so benignantly.

"O majestic friend," he murmured, addressing the Great Stone Face, "is not this man worthy to resemble thee?"

The face seemed to smile, but answered not a word.

Now it happened that the poet, though he dwelt so far away, had not only heard of Ernest, but had meditated much upon his character, until he deemed nothing so desirable as to meet this man, whose untaught wisdom walked hand in hand with the noble simplicity of his life. One summer morning, therefore, he took passage by the railroad, and, in the decline of the afternoon, alighted from the cars at no great distance from Ernest's cottage. The great hotel, which had formerly been the palace of Mr. Gathergold, was close at hand, but the poet, with his carpetbag on his arm, inquired at once where Ernest dwelt, and was resolved to be accepted as his guest.

Approaching the door, he there found the good old man, holding a volume in his hand, which alternately he read, and then, with a finger between the leaves, looked lovingly at the Great Stone Face.

"Good evening," said the poet. "Can you give a traveler a night's lodging?"

"Willingly," answered Ernest; and then he added, smiling, "Methinks I never saw the Great Stone Face look so hospitably at a stranger."

The poet sat down on the bench beside him, and he and Ernest talked together. The sympathies of these two men instructed them with a profounder sense than either could have attained alone. Their minds accorded into one strain, and made delightful music which neither of them could have claimed as all his own, nor distinguished his own share from the other's. They led one another, as it were, into a high pavilion of their thoughts, so remote, and hitherto so dim, that they had never entered it before, and so beautiful that they desired to be there always.

As Ernest listened to the poet, he imagined that the Great Stone Face was bending forward to listen too. He gazed earnestly into the poet's glowing eyes.

"Who are you, my strangely gifted guest?" he said.

The poet laid his finger on the volume that Ernest had been reading.

"You have read these poems," said he. "You know me, then, — for I wrote them."

Again, and still more earnestly than before, Ernest examined the poet's features; then turned towards the Great Stone Face; then back, with an uncertain aspect, to his guest. But his countenance fell; he shook his head, and sighed.

"Wherefore are you sad?" inquired the poet.

"Because," replied Ernest, "all through life I have awaited the fulfillment of a prophecy; and, when I read these poems, I hoped that it might be fulfilled in you."

"You hoped," answered the poet, faintly smiling, "to find in me the likeness of the Great Stone Face. And you are disappointed. For—in shame and sadness do I speak it, Ernest—I am not worthy to be typified by yonder benign and majestic image."

"And why?" asked Ernest. He pointed to the volume. "Are not those thoughts divine?"

"They have a strain of the Divinity," replied the poet. "You can hear in them the far-off echo of a heavenly song. But my life, dear Ernest, has not corresponded with my thought. I have had grand dreams, but they have been only dreams, because I have lived— and that, too, by my own choice—among poor and mean realities. Sometimes, even—shall I dare to say it?—I lack faith in the grandeur, the beauty, and the goodness, which my own works are said to have made more evident in Nature and in human life. Why, then, pure seeker of the good and true, shouldst thou hope to find me, in yonder image of the divine?"

The poet spoke sadly, and his eyes were dim with tears. So, likewise, were those of Ernest.

At the hour of sunset, as had long been his frequent custom, Ernest was to discourse to an assemblage of the neighboring inhabitants in the open air. He and the poet, arm in arm, still talking together as they went along, proceeded to the spot. It was a small nook among the hills, with a gray precipice behind. In another direction was seen the Great Stone Face, with the same cheer, combined with the same solemnity, in its benignant aspect.

Ernest began to speak, giving to the people of what was in his heart and mind. His words had power, because they accorded with his thoughts; and his thoughts had reality and depth, because they harmonized with the life which he had always lived. It was not mere breath that this preacher uttered; they were the words of life, because a life of good deeds and holy love was melted into them. Pearls, pure and rich, had been dissolved into this precious draught. The poet, as he listened, felt that the being and character of Ernest were a nobler strain of poetry than he had ever written. His eyes glistening with tears, he gazed reverentially at the venerable man, and said within himself that never was there an aspect so worthy of a prophet and a sage as that mild, sweet, thoughtful countenance, with the glory of white hair diffused about it. At a distance, but distinctly to be seen, high up in the golden light of the setting sun, appeared the Great Stone Face, with hoary mists around it, like the white hairs around the brow of Ernest. Its look of grand beneficence seemed to embrace the world.

At that moment, in sympathy with a thought which he was about to utter, the face of Ernest assumed a grandeur of expression, so imbued with benevolence, that the poet, by an irresistible impulse, threw his arms aloft and shouted:

"Behold! Behold! Ernest is himself the likeness of the Great Stone Face!"

Then all the people looked and saw that what the deep-sighted poet said was true. The prophecy was fulfilled. But Ernest, having finished what he had to say, took the poet's arm, and walked slowly homeward, still hoping that some wiser and better man than himself would by and by appear, bearing a resemblance to the Great Stone Face.

Nathaniel Hawthorne
1804–1864

THAT ALL OUR HOPE AND TRUST IS TO BE FIXED IN GOD ALONE

Lord, what is my confidence which I have in this life? Or what is the greatest comfort I can derive from any thing under Heaven?

Is it not thou, O Lord my God, whose mercies are without number?

Where hath it ever been well with me without Thee? Or when could it be ill with me, when Thou wert present?

I had rather be poor for Thee, than rich without Thee,

I rather choose to be a pilgrim on earth with Thee than without Thee to possess Heaven. Where Thou art, there is Heaven: and where Thou are not, there is death and hell.

Thou art all my desire, and therefore I must needs sigh and call and earnestly pray unto Thee,

In short there is none whom I can fully trust to, none that can seasonably help me in my necessities, but only Thou, my God.

Thou art my hope, Thou my confidence; Thou art my Comforter, and in all this most faithful unto me.

Thomas à Kempis

Crocodiles and Pandas

Only to you, O God, do we offer rafter-rattling
praise! We worship you with joyful noise and loud
reverence!
Only to you, O Holy One, does creation belong; only
to you do we owe our lives. Thanks be to God!
You are Divine Father and Eternal Mother; you anguish
over the transgressions and pain of all your children.

Upon your altar, O God, we place our troubled spirits;
at your holy table we confess:
Jealousy and harsh deceit have stained our hearts. We
have become people who exploit the helpless.
Without hesitation we plunder creation and tyrannize
the weak; each day we sentence the innocent to
lives of desolation.
Only your righteousness, O Shaper of History, can
cover our sin; your forgiveness stretches across the
dream-webbed reaches of space.

Standing in the ungentle sun of the marketplace, we
proclaim our repentance. No longer will we
pledge allegiance to the fat gods of prosperity.
No longer will we participate in destroying human
dignity; nor will we enslave ourselves to comfort
that is purchased at the expense of another's life.
We repent ourselves of power that bargains in cruelty;
we reject all vicious and slanderous speech.
Our public announcement is this: We will not auction
our heritage for gold and silver; nor will we accept
military strength in the place of Yahweh's
salvation-promise.

A ransomed and forgiven people, we are released for
   hope! You, O God, have brought us out of
   degradation into glory!
You keep watch through the night with those who
   grieve; you deliver the sin-ridden from their
   torment.
It is not in your nature, O Sustainer of All, to forsake
   your people. You will never abandon us to the
   immoderate appetites of evil.

Out of nothing you created ringed planets and thick
   moons. As a child scatters a handful of jacks, you
   dispersed galaxies across the rich, calm darkness.
You built up the mountain ranges and seeded the vine-
   tangled forests; from the morning mist you called
   forth monkeys and crocodiles and pandas.
Wisdom created the airless, blue-cold mass of glaciers;
   your hand shaped icy worlds that echo with the
   sounds of winters past.
With earth and sky as midwife, Yahweh birthed new
   possibility into being: And the divine birth pangs
   issued forth in humankind.

Walking in the hallowed paths of our ancestors, we
   bear witness to the staggering power and
   boundless generosity of creation.
The Spirit-filled ones sense now the rejoicing of rocks
   and the soaring harmony of eagles. Blessed are
   those who perceive the reflection of Ultimate
   Energy in a silent smile.
You are at work, O God, bending each vulnerable
   moment to your unearthly purpose. You demolish
   the gray walls that separate creation from itself.
In this historical moment, O Holy One, you are
   tearing down the barbed wire erected by sin.
   Incarnate Destiny is overturning the rule of death.

Let us dedicate ourselves to the newborn day! Let us
celebrate the Hallelujah-morning of forgiveness!
Sing out with resolute voice: Yahweh at last has set the
captives free!
If your voice is silent, clap your hands: Despair is
already routed!
If you are unable to hear, stamp your feet: Steadfast
love has vanquished death!
If your feet cannot move, feel the atoms within you
rejoicing: All life belongs to the Life-giver!
Thanks be to God!

Martin Bell

HOW TO HELP
HURTING PEOPLE

A simple prayer, a Scripture that has meant something to you, these can be a great comfort to a hurting person. The Word of God is where we "find grace to help us in our time of need" (Hebrews 4:16).

Rather than giving personal advice, how much better would it be for Christians to share God's loving promises. It is a comfort to hear the words of God in times of stress. If you have problems remembering proper verses, there are some fine little booklets that you can carry in your pocket or purse which give verses for many different situations.

I remember a time in my late teens when I had a case of "puppy love," which was very real to the "puppy." We were even talking about marriage, although we were both much too young. However, she felt the Lord was leading her to another young man who was one of my best friends. I felt like my heart would break, so I went to a clergyman friend of mine for help. He turned to 2 Corinthians 1:3–4, 6. The passage not only tells us we are comforted in our trials, but that our trials can equip us to comfort others. I was comforted by those words of the Apostle Paul, just as many others have been. The Lord knew that young romance was not His will for my life, and that I would find in Ruth the perfect wife for me.

An overdose of Scripture at the wrong time may do more harm than good. Hearing verses on "counting trials as joy," in the midst of someone's difficulty can be like throwing gasoline on a fire or rubbing salt in a wound. A person needs time to assimilate what has happened, to assess the physical or emotional damage. Hearing something like "God must love you very much to put you through this," is not the bandage a person needs.

We need to build trust through listening, through caring in a tangible way. Perhaps your friend doesn't know the Lord, and you feel awkward bringing up the subject of God as the one who comforts perfectly. You might say, "I wish I could do more for you. When you feel like it, let me take you to lunch."

If you cannot find examples in your life that might relate to a sufferer, the perfect example is Jesus. He experienced people who betrayed Him. He knows what it is like to suffer. You can explain how your hurting friend can have a relationship with Him. Pray for the right words, pray for the way to comfort. Pray, don't preach.

Those who have suffered most are often best able to comfort others. I know of pastors whose ministries have been enriched by suffering. Through their trials they have learned to live through the difficulties of people in their church family.

Someone who has experienced the same sort of pain is the one who can minister best. However, to say, "I know how you feel," is usually an unnecessary and frequently unwelcome approach. No one knows exactly how another feels. One couple who had lost their oldest son in an accident tried to comfort another couple whose child had died after lingering for many months. The comfort was only in the loss, not in the circumstances. Better to say, "I don't know how you feel, I can't really put myself in your shoes, but this is how I was comforted . . ." Our sufferings may be hard to bear, but they teach us lessons which, in turn, equip and enable us to help others.

Only God's spirit can truly mend a broken heart, but we can be a part of the healing process. We don't have to be a priest or preacher, a trained counselor or psychiatrist to be a comforter. We just need to be available, as Christ is available to us. When He was comforting His disciples before He left them, they were confused, questioning, and frightened. He said, "Now is your time of grief, but I will see you again and you will rejoice, and no one will take away your joy" (John 16:22).

Our attitude toward suffering should not be, "Grit your teeth and bear it," hoping it will pass as quickly as possible. Our goal should be to learn all we can from our personal problems, so that we can fulfill a ministry of comfort, just as Jesus did. "Because he himself suffered when he was tempted, he is able to help those who are being tempted" (Hebrews 2:18).

Billy Graham

ASK GOD FOR A
STRONGER HOPE

"Now the God of hope fill you with all joy and peace in believing, that ye may abound in hope, through the power of the Holy Ghost" (Romans 15:13). God is the God of hope; not only of the first seed but also of the whole growth and harvest of it in us. He does not give a saint the first grace of conversion and then leave the completion of it wholly to his human skill.

Be sure you humbly acknowledge God by constantly waiting on Him for your spiritual growth. "The young lions" are said to "seek their meat from God" (Psalm 104:21). God has taught them to express their wants when they are hungry; and by this they have learned that their Maker is also their Supplier. At first a baby expresses his needs only by crying; but as soon as he knows who his mother is, he directs his cries to her.

The Father can always find you, Christian. He knows what you want but He waits to supply you until you cry to Him. Does God care for the beasts in the field? Then surely He will care for you, His child in His house. You might pray for more riches and be denied; but a prayer for more grace is sure to be answered quickly.

Love has a secret yet powerful influence on hope. Moses befriended the Israelite when he killed the Egyptian who had fought with him. And love kills slavish fear—one of the worst enemies hope has—and thereby strengthens hope's hand. Whoever pulls up the weeds helps the corn to grow. It is fear that oppresses the Christian's spirit so that he cannot act or hope strongly. "Perfect love casteth out fear" (1 John 4:18). The freewoman will cast out the bondwoman. Fear is one of Hagar's breed—an affection that keeps everyone in bondage who partakes of it.

Love cannot tolerate fear. The loving soul asks, "Can I fear that the One who loves me most will ever hurt me? Fear and doubt, away with you! There is no room for you in my heart." Charity "thinketh no evil" (1 Corinthians 13:5).

William Gurnall

OUR HOPE IS IN HEAVEN

The Christian's occupation is heavenly. That is to say, God is our overseer. We may plant our seeds here on earth, but our crop will be harvested in heaven. This keeps our hearts and desires on a celestial plane. In a spiritual sense, the Christian's feet stand where other man cannot even see. He treads on the moon and is clothed with the sun. He looks down on earthly men as one from a high hill looks upon those living in a swamp. While he breathes in pure heavenly air, they are suffocating in a fog of carnal pleasures and profits. He knows one heavenly pearl is worth infinitely more than the earthly accumulation of a whole lifetime.

The great business of a saint's life is to be doing things that enlarge the kingdom of heaven. Not only is he interested in his own welfare, but he eagerly recruits his friends and neighbors to join in his eternal enterprise. Now this alarms hell. What! Not content to go to heaven himself, but by his holy example and faithful work will he try to carry them along with him also? This brings the lion raging out of his den. Such a Christian, to be sure, will find the devil in his way to oppose him.

The Christian's hopes are all heavenly. He does not expect lasting satisfaction from anything the world has to offer. Indeed, he would think himself the most miserable person to have ever lived, if the only rewards he could expect from his religion were on this side of eternity. No, it is heaven and eternal life that he anticipates. And though he is so poor that he cannot leave one cent in his will, yet he counts himself a greater heir than if he were a child of the greatest prince on earth.

Hope is the grace that shows us how to rejoice in the prospect of promised glory. It sits beside us in the worst of times. When things are so bad that we cannot imagine how they could possibly get worse, hope lifts our eyes from our immediate troubles and places them on our future eternal joys.

William Gurnall

LOVE AND CHARITY

Love is a deep personal feeling for others. Christian love includes being loyal to others and taking responsibility for others. Jesus showed love clearly by his concern and care for others and by his life and death. We show our love for Jesus by taking care of God's creation, including other people.

"You have heard it said, 'Love your neighbor and hate your enemy.' But I tell you: Love your enemies and pray for those who persecute you that you may be sons of your Father in heaven. He causes his sun to rise on the evil and the good, and sends rain on the righteous and the unrighteous. If you love those who love you, what reward will you get? Are not even the tax collectors doing that? And if you greet only your brothers, what are you doing more than others? Do not even pagans do that? Be perfect, therefore, as your heavenly Father is perfect."

Matthew 5:43-48

LOVE—A LANGUAGE
EVERYONE UNDERSTANDS

God knew that love is a language everyone understands, so he sent Jesus into the world. In Jesus Christ we see the incarnation of love. He appeals to people of all ages, of all races, of all clans— because they see in him love.

There is no word in any language today that deserves more attention than this little four-letter word—*l o v e*. The extent of its application into today's world determines the future of humankind. Basic in every marriage bond, essential in all lasting friendships, necessary in all relationships—this word holds the key to that brave new world of which we dream and toward which we strive.

It was because of this that Paul said, "So faith, hope, love abide, these three; but the greatest of these is love." Wherefore, "Make love your aim" (I Cor. 13:13–14:1 RSV). This is the supreme virtue.

Paul was right. Life's greatest virtue is love. And Jesus Christ is the incarnation of love, the highest expression of it we know, and he commanded his disciples that they should love one another. He insisted that his followers be known by their love for him and for one another. Jesus came not to lay down a set of rules for human behavior but to manifest a spirit, a new way of life. Without this spirit of love, life is incomplete, imperfect, and defective.

Let us look at this love which completes life and crowns it.

In the first place, *knowledge without love leads to evil ends and even destruction.* Paul says, "I may prophesy, fathom all mysteries and secret lore, . . . but if I have no love, I count for nothing" (Vs. 2). He is telling us that knowledge, learning, and scientific progress, avail for nothing unless at the heart there is good will toward all people.

How true his words are today! We have explored the mysteries of life. We have fashioned in laboratories that which can lengthen life. We have conquered the air with planes and the sea with ships and submarines. We have shortened space and to some degree lengthened time with our labor-saving devices. Our world has been squeezed into a neighborhood through the machine.

Yet, what has happened? In our laboratory where vaccines

have been produced to lengthen men's lives, we have turned them into gases which would shorten them. Our planes which have conquered the air and have borne medicine and food for people in need, now threaten the existence of millions. Where once they carried life, they now carry the possibility of death. Ships which connected continents and brought them closer together have been used in our time to push them farther apart.

Paul says that we may prophesy, understand all mysteries and secret lore, but unless there is love in the heart, that which we have made counts for nothing except destruction. It is not enough to gain wisdom, but that wisdom must be directed by a loving will.

In the second place, *love is a contribution everyone can make.* We should never be tempted to underestimate the importance of that which we can add to the enrichment of life, however small it might seem to us. As someone has said, one bucketful of water will not quench a raging fire, but the principle is right, and many bucketfuls will do it.

Our lives are placed in a system of relations and into that web we each can pour our contribution of love and good will. It is like dropping a pebble into a still pool. No section of that pool is undisturbed by the movement.

Love is a contribution all can make. We can love one another in the church, in our homes, in our business, and at our play. We can let go from our lives the light of love lighted by the central sun, *Jesus Christ,* from whose energy we draw our light. We can refuse to hate when others have abused us. We can enlarge our circle of love by including people we do not like.

And finally, the *future* belongs to love. It belongs to love because it is a language everyone can understand and that everyone can speak. The future belongs to love because it enriches the person who gives it as well as the person who receives it. But even more, the future belongs to love because it belongs to God, and God is love. All hatred, falsehood, fear, cruelty, enmity, and bitterness are doomed by love. The resurrection of Christ is the symbol telling us that victory belongs to love, that evil and hatred cannot hold sway over it.

Wallace Fridy

From: *The Vision of Sir Launfal*

The Holy Supper is kept, indeed,
In whatso we share with another's need;
Not what we give, but what we share,
For the gift without the giver is bare;
Who gives himself with his alms feeds three,
Himself, his hungering neighbor, and me.

James Russell Lowell

A MERRY CHRISTMAS

Jo was the first to wake in the gray dawn of Christmas morning. No stockings hung at the fireplace, and for a moment she felt as much disappointed as she did long ago, when her little sock fell down because it was so crammed with goodies. Then she remembered her mother's promise, and slipping her hand under her pillow, drew out a little crimson-covered book. She knew it very well, for it was that beautiful old story of the best life ever lived, and Jo felt that it was a true guidebook for any pilgrim going the long journey. She woke Meg with a "Merry Christmas" and bade her see what was under her pillow. A green-covered book appeared, with the same picture inside, and a few words written by their mother, which made their one present very precious in their eyes. Presently Beth and Amy woke, to rummage and find their little books also—one dove-colored, the other blue; and all sat looking at and talking about them, while the east grew rosy with the coming day.

In spite of her small vanities, Margaret had a sweet and pious nature, which unconsciously influenced her sisters, especially Jo, who loved her very tenderly, and obeyed her because her advice was so gently given.

"Girls," said Meg seriously, looking from the tumbled head beside her to the two little nightcapped ones in the room beyond, "Mother wants us to read and love and mind these books, and we must begin at once. We used to be faithful about it, but since father went away, and all this war trouble unsettled us, we have neglected many things. You can do as you please, but *I* shall keep my book on the table here and read a little every morning as soon as I wake, for I know it will do me good and help me through the day."

Then she opened her new book and began to read. Jo put her arm around her, and, leaning cheek to cheek read also, with the quiet expression so seldom seen on her restless face.

"How good Meg is! Come, Amy, let's do as they do. I'll help you with the hard words, and they'll explain things if we don't understand," whispered Beth, very much impressed by the pretty books and her sisters' example.

"I'm glad mine is blue," said Amy. And then the rooms were very still while the pages were softly turned, and the winter sunshine crept in to touch the bright heads and serious faces with a Christmas greeting.

"Where is Mother?" asked Meg, as she and Jo ran down to thank her for their gifts, half an hour later.

"Goodness only knows. Some poor creeter come a-beggin', and your ma went straight off to see what was needed. There never *was* such a woman for givin' away vittles and drink, clothes and firin'," replied Hannah, who had lived with the family since Meg was born, and was considered by them all more as a friend than a servant.

"She will be back soon, I think, so fry your cakes, and have everything ready," said Meg, looking over the presents which were collected in a basket and kept under the sofa, ready to be produced at the proper time. "Why, where is Amy's bottle of cologne?" she added, as the little flask did not appear.

"She took it out a minute ago, and went off with it to put a ribbon on it, or some such notion," replied Jo, dancing about the room to take the first stiffness off the new army slippers.

"How nice my handkerchiefs look, don't they? Hannah washed and ironed them for me, and I marked them all myself," said Beth, looking proudly at the somewhat uneven letters which had cost her such labor.

"Bless the child! She's gone and put 'Mother' on them instead of 'M. March.' How funny!" cried Jo, taking up one.

"Isn't it right? I thought it was better to do it so, because Meg's initials are 'M. M.,' and I don't want anyone to use these but Marmee," said Beth, looking troubled.

"It's all right, dear, and a very pretty idea—quite sensible, too, for no one can ever mistake now. It will please her very much, I know," said Meg, with a frown for Jo and a smile for Beth.

"There's Mother. Hide the basket, quick!" cried Jo, as a door slammed, and steps sounded in the hall.

Amy came in hastily, and looked rather abashed when she saw her sisters all waiting for her.

"Where have you been, and what are you hiding behind you?"

asked Meg, surprised to see, by her hood and cloak, that lazy Amy had been out so early.

"Don't laugh at me, Jo! I didn't mean anyone should know till the time came. I only meant to change the little bottle for a big one, and I gave *all* my money to get it, and I'm truly trying not to be selfish any more."

As she spoke, Amy showed the handsome flask which replaced the cheap one, and looked so earnest and humble in her little effort to forget herself that Meg hugged her on the spot, and Jo pronounced her "a trump," while Beth ran to the window, and picked her finest rose to ornament the stately bottle.

"You see I felt ashamed of my present, after reading and talking about being good this morning, so I ran round the corner and changed it the minute I was up: and I'm *so* glad, for mine is the handsomest now."

Another bang of the street door sent the basket under the sofa, and the girls to the table, eager for breakfast.

"Merry Christmas, Marmee! Many of them! Thank you for our books; we read some, and mean to every day," they cried, in chorus.

"Merry Christmas, little daughters! I'm glad you began at once, and hope you will keep on. But I want to say one word before we sit down. Not far away from here lies a poor woman with a little newborn baby. Six children are huddled into one bed to keep from freezing, for they have no fire. There is nothing to eat over there, and the oldest boy came to tell me they were suffering hunger and cold. My girls, will you give them your breakfast as a Christmas present?"

They were all unusually hungry, having waited nearly an hour, and for a minute no one spoke—only a minute, for Jo exclaimed impetuously, "I'm so glad you came before we began!"

"May I go and help carry the things to the poor little children?" asked Beth eagerly.

"*I* shall take the cream and the muffins," added Amy, heroically giving up the articles she most liked.

Meg was already covering the buckwheats, and piling the bread into one big plate.

"I thought you'd do it," said Mrs. March, smiling as if satisfied. "You shall all go and help me, and when we come back we will have bread and milk for breakfast, and make it up at dinnertime."

They were soon ready, and the procession set out. Fortunately it was early, and they went through back streets, so few people saw them, and no one laughed at the queer party.

A poor, bare, miserable room it was, with broken windows, no fire, ragged bedclothes, a sick mother, wailing baby, and a group of pale, hungry children cuddled under one old quilt, trying to keep warm.

How the big eyes stared and the blue lips smiled as the girls went in!

"*Ach, mein Gott!* It is good angels come to us!" said the poor woman, crying for joy.

"Funny angels in hoods and mittens," said Jo, and set them laughing.

In a few minutes it really did seem as if kind spirits had been at work there. Hannah, who had carried wood, made a fire, and stopped up the broken panes with old hats and her own cloak. Mrs. March gave the mother tea and gruel, and comforted her with promises of help, while she dressed the little baby as tenderly as if it had been her own. The girls, meantime, spread the table, set the children round the fire, and fed them like so many hungry birds — laughing, talking, and trying to understand the funny broken English.

"*Das ist gut!*" "*Die Engel-kinder!*" cried the poor things, as they ate and warmed their purple hands at the comfortable blaze.

The girls had never been called angel children before, and thought it very agreeable, especially Jo, who had been considered a "Sancho" ever since she was born. That was a very happy breakfast, though they didn't get any of it; and when they went away, leaving comfort behind, I think there were not in all the city four merrier people than the hungry little girls who gave away their breakfasts and contented themselves with bread and milk on Christmas morning.

Louisa May Alcott, in
Little Women

Love in Action

Truth proclaims it; love the wonder healer —
No blemish left, if that herb is used.
As God wished, the world was shaped in love.
Revealed to Moses, it was the best of things,
Heaven's image, priceless, the plant of peace.
But heaven could not contain the weight of love,
Till, here on earth, it fed to the full, took
Flesh and blood. After that, no leaf there was
On tree so light as love, mobile in air, plunging
As a needle point, no steel could stop it,
Nor castle wall. So, on earth as in heaven,
Love leads God's people, like a mayor,
Agent between the commons and the king. Love
Directs all, frames law, fixes fines
For the people's crimes. Know it for sure,
Love comes surging from the power of God,
Its source, its mountain spring, the human heart.

From Piers Plowman *by William Langland*
1330?–1400?
Translated by Ronald Tamplin

FRIEND OR ENEMY?

As a boy growing up in West Virginia, I wanted to make some spending money for myself. So I tried selling flower seeds, greeting cards, the *Grit* newspaper, Cloverine salve, and finally, I became a newsboy selling the morning and evening newspapers.

The thing I disliked most about my job was that it interfered with my sleep in the morning and my play in the afternoon. I also disliked dealing with the dogs. I never really learned how to handle them. I tried rocks, sticks, a water pistol, a flashlight in the mornings, and a gruff voice. But how gruff can a thirteen-year-old boy, whose voice is in the process of changing, sound?

A few years ago I heard about a letter carrier who also had to deal with the dogs. Instead of hitting them or threatening them or running from them, he decided to feed them. He carried a box of dog food and fed about eighteen dogs a day. I either made enemies of the dogs or, at best, kept my distance. He made friends.

Maybe there is a lesson to be learned in that. Life is filled with people who threaten us in one way or another. We can deal violently with them, scream at them, or ignore them. Could we not learn to "feed" them?

The best way to get rid of an enemy is to make a friend of that person. We can keep fighting if we desire, but God has asked us to make friends of our enemies. Are you ready to try?

Jerry Hayner

WHY THE EVERGREEN TREES NEVER LOSE THEIR LEAVES

Winter was coming, and the birds had flown far to the south, where the air was warm and they could find berries to eat. One little bird had broken its wing and could not fly with the others. It was alone in the cold world of frost and snow. The forest looked warm, and it made its way to the trees as well as it could, to ask for help.

First it came to a birch tree. "Beautiful birch tree," it said, "my wing is broken, and my friends have flown away. May I live among your branches till they come back to me?"

"No, indeed," answered the birch tree, drawing her fair green leaves away. "We of the great forest have our own birds to help. I can do nothing for you."

"The birch is not very strong," said the little bird to itself, "and it might be that she could not hold me easily. I will ask the oak." So the bird said: "Great oak tree, you are so strong, will you not let me live on your boughs till my friends come back in the spring-time?"

"In the springtime!" cried the oak. "That is a long way off. How do I know what you might do in all that time? Birds are always looking for something to eat, and you might even eat up some of my acorns."

"It may be that the willow will be kind to me," thought the bird, and it said: "Gentle willow, my wing is broken, and I could not fly to the south with the other birds. May I live on your branches till the springtime?"

The willow did not look gentle then, for she drew herself up proudly and said: "Indeed, I do not know you, and we willows never talk to people whom we do not know. Very likely there are trees somewhere that will take in strange birds. Leave me at once."

The poor little bird did not know what to do. Its wing was not yet strong, but it began to fly away as well as it could. Before it had gone far a voice was heard. "Little bird," it said, "where are you going?"

"Indeed, I do not know," answered the bird sadly. "I am very cold."

"Come right here, then, " said the friendly spruce tree, for it was her voice that had called. "You shall live on my warmest branch all winter if you choose."

"Will you really let me?" asked the little bird eagerly.

"Indeed, I will," answered the kind-hearted spruce tree. "If your friends have flown away, it is time for the trees to help you. Here is the branch where my leaves are thickest and softest."

"My branches are not very thick," said the friendly pine tree, "but I am big and strong, and I can keep the North Wind from you and the spruce."

"I can help, too," said a little juniper tree. "I can give you berries all winter long, and every bird knows that juniper berries are good."

So the spruce gave the lonely little bird a home; the pine kept the cold North Wind away from it; and the juniper gave it berries to eat. The other trees looked on and talked together wisely.

"I would not have strange birds on my boughs," said the birch.

"I shall not give my acorns away for any one," said the oak.

"I never have anything to do with strangers," said the willow, and the three trees drew their leaves closely about them.

In the morning all those shining, green leaves lay on the ground, for a cold North Wind had come in the night, and every leaf that it touched fell from the tree.

"May I touch every leaf in the forest?" asked the wind in its frolic.

"No," said the Frost King. "The trees that have been kind to the little bird with the broken wing may keep their leaves."

This is why the leaves of the spruce, the pine, and the juniper are always green.

Florence Holbrook

THE LOVELIEST ROSE
IN THE WORLD

Once there reigned a queen, in whose garden were found the most glorious flowers at all seasons and from all the lands of the world. But more than all others she loved the roses, and she had many kinds of this flower, from the wild dog-rose with its apple-scented green leaves to the most splendid, large, crimson roses. They grew against the garden walls, wound themselves around the pillars and wind-frames, and crept through the windows into the rooms, and all along the ceilings in the halls. And the roses were of many colors, and of every fragrance and form.

But care and sorrow dwelt in those halls. The queen lay upon a sick-bed, and the doctors said she must die.

"There is still one thing that can save her," said the wise man. "Bring her the loveliest rose in the world, the rose that is the symbol of the purest, the brightest love. If that is held before her eyes ere they close, she will not die."

Then old and young came from every side with roses, the loveliest that bloomed in each garden, but they were not of the right sort. The flower was to be plucked from the Garden of Love. But what rose in all that garden expressed the highest and purest love? And the poets sang of the loveliest rose in the world—of the love of maid and youth, and of the love of dying heroes.

"But they have not named the right flower," said the wise man. "They have not pointed out the place where it blooms in its splendor. It is not the rose that springs from the hearts of youthful lovers, though this rose will ever be fragrant in song. It is not the bloom that sprouts from the blood flowing from the breast of the hero who dies for his country, though few deaths are sweeter than his, and no rose is redder than the blood that flows then. Nor is it the wondrous flower to which man devotes many a sleepless night and much of his fresh life—the magic flower of science."

"But I know where it blooms," said a happy mother, who came with her pretty child to the bedside of the dying queen. "I know where the loveliest rose of love may be found. It springs in the blooming cheeks of my sweet child, when, waking from sleep, it opens its eyes and smiles tenderly at me."

"Lovely is this rose, but there is a lovelier still," said the wise man.

"I have seen the loveliest, purest rose that blooms," said a woman. "I saw it on the cheeks of the queen. She had taken off her golden crown. And in the long, dreary night she carried her sick child in her arms. She wept, kissed it, and prayed for her child."

"Holy and wonderful is the white rose of a mother's grief," answered the wise man, "but it is not the one we seek."

"The loveliest rose in the world I saw at the altar of the Lord," said the good Bishop, "the young maidens went to the Lord's Table. Roses were blushing and pale roses shining on their fresh cheeks. A young girl stood there. She looked with all the love and purity of her spirit up to heaven. That was the expression of the highest and purest love."

"May she be blessed," said the wise man, "but not one of you has yet named the loveliest rose in the world."

Then there came into the room a child, the queen's little son.

"Mother," cried the boy, "only hear what I have read."

And the child sat by the bedside and read from the Book of Him who suffered death upon the cross to save men, and even those who were not yet born. "Greater love there is not."

And a rosy glow spread over the cheeks of the queen, and her eyes gleamed, for she saw that from the leaves of the Book there bloomed the loveliest rose, that sprang from the blood of Christ shed on the cross.

"I see it!" she said, "he who beholds this, the loveliest rose on earth, shall never die."

Hans Christian Andersen (Adapted)

WATER FROM THE ROCK

A part of my springtime experience has always been the spring cleaning of irrigation ditches that carry water to the fields. Some ditches require more cleaning than others. But no matter how well a ditch is engineered or how well it is managed it requires some cleaning. Silt, debris, last year's weeds or leaves, erosion caused by farm animals—there is always something that will need to be cleaned out or repaired before the ditch will carry its maximum flow. Keeping some ditches in repair can be very hard work.

Cleaning ditches seems to me to be similar to the exercise of the Christian life. . . . God gives his love freely, even as the snow melts on the mountains and the streams flow freely toward the sea. To the Christian there is given the challenge of being a channel for God's love. We do our part to cause it to "flow upon, over, and through" a parched and thirsty world.

We cannot keep the water of life flowing through a channel that is blocked by trash. We cannot repair the broken places until the trash is cleaned out. And, for the very reason that the ditch of my life flows through woods where there are living things, the work of cleaning it is never finished. I can never fix it once and for all, any more than I can say my prayers or give my love once and for all. Every summer brings its new crop of leaves and weeds; each fall the cattle come off the hills, and any night the beavers may move in. While there is life I shall be cleaning ditches—mending broken places, cleaning out trash. It is hard work. But I shall also know the joy of seeing thirsty land turned into green pastures and desert places producing crops for hungry people.

Don Ian Smith
from Sagebrush Seed

FAITH AND LOVE

I am not afraid to maintain publicly and candidly that the apostle, in this thirteenth chapter of the First Letter to the Corinthians, means nothing the least bit different in his entire discourse from what we call saving faith. This he calls love, and distinguishes it in the last verse of the chapter from faith purely for the reason that as soon as one has a faithful heart toward the Savior, one must trust in certain things and promises which one sees neither now nor then, but must expect. These things, when they are fulfilled, take away that part of saving faith which consists in hoping and expecting, and leave nothing behind except that part which consists in love and faithfulness.

O dear friends, do not imagine that we know the Savior. We begin to know Him only when we have loved Him very tenderly, when we have loved Him first above all things, when for us nothing in the world is in competition with Him; when we have forgotten ourselves, our health, our life, our possessions and goods, our enjoyment on account of Him. Our whole life consists in the increasing and growing in knowledge of Him, so that we know Him better today than yesterday, and in a year know Him a year better; in twenty years twenty years better, and in eternity an eternity better than now. This is the great science. In Him and His Person lies hidden a treasure of wisdom and knowledge which cannot be fathomed or exhausted.

Count Von Zinzendorf
1700–1760

Our Mother's Way

Oft within a little cottage,
As the shadows gently fall,
While the sunlight touches softly,
One sweet face upon the wall,
There the lonely loved ones gather,
And in hushed and tender tone,
Ask each other's full forgiveness,
For the wrong that each had done.

As I wondered why this custom,
At the closing of the day,
"Tis because" they sweetly answered,
"It was once our mother's way."

If our home is bright and cheery,
If it holds a welcome true,
Opening wide its door of greeting,
To the many—not the few;
If we share our Father's bounty,
With the needy day by day,
'Tis because our hearts remember,
"This was ever mother's way."

Sometimes when our hearts grow weary,
Or our task seems very long,
When our burdens look too heavy,
And we deem the right all wrong,
Then we gain a new fresh courage,
As once more we rise to say,
Let us do our duty bravely,
"This was our dear mother's way."

O how oft it comes before us,
That sweet face upon the wall,
And her memory seems more precious,
As we on her Savior call
That at last, when evening shadows,
Mark the closing of life's day,
They may find us calmly waiting,
To go home our mother's way.

Gentle mother, loving mother,
Sainted mother fond and true,
Resting now in peace with Jesus
Loving hearts remember you.

James McGranhan,
1885

PUTTIN' ON THE DOG

My grandmother took great joy in teaching me what the Scriptures have to say about being hospitable. "The Bible says, we're to practice hospitality ungrudgingly to one another" (I Peter 4:9), she explained the day she dropped everything to feed a hungry family of ten who "just happened to be in town." But each year when the calendar turns to July, I smile at the memory of an unexpected lesson we *both* once learned about being neighborly.

How well I remember the Fourth of July weekend our hospitality got a little out of hand. I had just started nursing school and practically lived at my grandparents' home. It was then my thrifty Grandpa decided he could save the whole neighborhood a bundle of money by purchasing a community blood pressure kit. Each Saturday morning the local menfolk would congregate on the shady front porch of my grandparents' stone cottage to get their blood pressures checked. Grandma would serve up a tray of coffee and oven-warmed cobbler to the motley gathering of retirees . . . all dressed in flannel shirts and gray or green work pants, even on the hottest of days.

One Saturday we spotted Mr. Chang, the new next-door neighbor, checking his mailbox. "C'mon over and get your blood pressured checked," Grandpa hollered. "Our granddaughter here's studying to be a nurse. Won't cost you a dime. Cobbler and coffee's on the house, too."

A slow smile spread across Mr. Chang's face, a smile as sunny as the marigolds edging my grandparents' walkway. I stood up from the creaky glider to get an even better look at the elderly man in the blazing floral shirt who lived in the little rental house all by himself. For several weeks now, I'd studied his curious habits from a distance. Every morning he'd use a small plastic tumbler to water the flowers in his hanging baskets. Then he'd trot back through the bright orange door a half dozen times to refill it. I'd heard one of the neighbor ladies mention that he'd recently opened a Chinese restaurant—one of those fascinating places with "atmosphere" where they used real linen napkins and drew curtains around you so you could eat in total privacy.

Mr. Chang shuffled across the yard and leaned against the

porch bannister. "Say we have a nurse in the neighborhood?" he inquired. "Think I'm gonna like living here." He pointed to his white bungalow and took off back down the stairs in fast little steps, whistling. A few moments later he reappeared, passing around a plate of fortune cookies. "For all of you," he said slowly and distinctly, his gold upper front tooth glistening. "I have the very good fortune to be your new neighbor."

Every few days after that, Mr. Chang showed up at the back door, usually with a carry-out carton of something strangely delicious from his restaurant. "Trade Chang's specialty for a jar of Grandpa's green beans?" he'd offer with a sparkling smile. Then he'd settle into a yellow vinyl chair at the gray Formica table and talk to Grandma as she buzzed about preparing a covered dish for one of her many church suppers. "Sure you don't want some of Chang's famous eggroll to take to church?" he'd tease as he sipped iced tea.

If Mr. Chang had a tear in one of his shirts or a restaurant table cloth that needed mending, the two of them would retreat to Grandma's makeshift alterations shop, located just off the kitchen in the dining room. With the hum of her Singer and his soft whistling, everything would be as good as new within minutes. "Your son is in service, too?" he asked Grandpa one day as he studied the framed family photos on the buffet. "My boys also fight for American freedom. I so proud of them I hang their military pictures in the restaurant. I *love* this America."

Sometimes Mr. Chang would spy a heaping plate of my home-baked chocolate chip cookies on the counter, or a jar of Grandma's strawberry preserves shimmering in the organdy-curtained window facing the side of his house. He'd rarely leave empty handed, or without instructions to come back and see us soon. And he always left as cheerful as the whistling tea kettle on Grandma's stove.

On July 4th weekend when we were putting up the flag, Grandma got a brainstorm, as she called it. "You're in college now, Roberta, and I don't believe you've ever cooked an entire meal on your own. I think you ought to invite Mr. Chang over here for dinner—a nice sitdown affair. He's not just a new neighbor, you know," she whispered confidentially. "He's a new citizen in our country, too. Why don't we ask him to celebrate the Fourth of July with us?"

I ripped out a page from a composition notebook and began making a list. "Chinese cuisine, don't you think?" I asked as excitement spilled like flour from Grandma's sifter. "I'll call Aunt Bette and get the recipe for that beef chow mein she makes."

I researched the proper way to set a table, and quickly surveyed the dining room. Grandma's lace tablecloth and embroidered napkins might work, but we'd definitely need some better dishes. Grandma's "crystal" consisted of peanut butter jars and a few odd pieces of glassware from yard sales; her "china" was hopelessly outdated Fiestaware. I made a beeline for the telephone. Yes, Flo down at the church would loan us some silver serving dishes, and Harriet would be glad to let us borrow the wonderful bone china she'd inherited from her sister-in-law. I'd look for some chopsticks at the five-and-dime.

A gentle breeze ruffled the curtains, almost mocking our kitchen frenzy. Only the best would do for Mr. Chang, and nothing we owned now seemed good enough. I scoured Grandma's metal kitchen cabinet for the makings of a new centerpiece, rummaging through pots and pans, plastic cupcake ornaments, and paper flags on toothpicks. I finally decided to give a tired bowl of plastic fruit that Midas touch with some gold spray paint.

With a list as long as Grandma's kitchen counter, I took off for the grocery store, my babysitting savings and Grandma's entire week's food allowance stashed in my wallet. Anything that vaguely resembled "Chinese" got tossed in the buggy. Aunt Bette had stressed a cheaper cut of meat would do just fine—after all, I'd be marinating it in vegetable oil and soy sauce over night. But I opted for the top cut of sirloin, way over our budget. I picked up a few fresh green peppers, too. Sure, there were plenty in Grandpa's garden, but we needed *better* peppers for this occasion.

Back in Grandma's kitchen, Grandpa shook his head as I stacked cans of fancy Chinese vegetables and noodles by the sink. "This looks like someone else's kitchen," he grumbled, rattling pots and pans. "Where'd you hide the loaf of bread? Or don't we eat plain white bread around here anymore? Count *me* out of this foolishness."

Come July 4th afternoon, the dining room looked like a fine restaurant and bore no resemblance to Grandma's alterations shop. Coats and dresses that once hung on old-fashioned wall lamps and bolts of fabric stored on the buffet were safely tucked away in closets or under beds. "It'll take us two weeks to find everything again," Grandma declared. "But that's okay. You need to learn to do this!"

The table was set to perfection, complete with candlelight, when the bell rang. "I never knew fixing a meal could be so much work," I muttered to Grandma as we headed for the door. I was already dreaming of hitting the sofa as soon as the ordeal was over. There in the doorway stood Mr. Chang, shooting the breeze with Grandpa, dressed to our astonishment in a barbecue apron, with sunglasses in his shirt pocket.

Totally exhausted, I gestured toward the dining room. I raised the lid on the fresh polished silver serving dish to pronounce the completion of my twelve hours of labor. "Voila!" (I'd heard that phrase on TV and, besides, I didn't know any Chinese.) *"Beef chow mein!"*

A look of confusion crossed Mr. Chang's face as he scratched his balding head. "I thought I come for good ol' American picnic—not Chinese. You go to all this trouble *for me*? Not necessary. *What you are is quite enough.*"

"We wanted to make you feel at home by cooking food *you're* used to," I tried to explain.

"I feel at home since the first day I discover all of you," he answered. "And you, my young American friend, you look so tired, like you stay up all night and cook."

"I don't know about you, Chang, but I'm fixing me some of this good ol' country cookin'," Grandpa said. "Like a slice of apple pie and ice cream." Mr. Chang's face lit up, and he shuffled behind Grandpa. Grandma and I tarried at the table, taking in our dining disaster.

"What will we ever do with all of this food? And these chopsticks, Grandma?"

"Don't worry, I'll take it all down to my class meeting at church tomorrow night. It'll be quite a treat for the ladies." A smile broke across her softly wrinkled face. "I'm leading the Bible study on hospitality. I've been wondering all week what I could use for an illustration. Now I know."

Grandma motioned toward the icebox where all the fixin's for our own abandoned Fourth of July Picnic were stored—watermelon, potato salad, frankfurters. "Put a few hot dogs on the grill, will you, Mr. Chang?" I called out the back door with a new surge of energy. I grabbed a red checked tablecloth, some paper plates and napkins, plastic utensils, and a handful of paper flags from the kitchen cabinet. Right in our own back yard a much wiser and joyous interpretation of 1 Peter 4:9 was in progress, all on the spur of the moment.

In the future when I ask someone over, I'm going to just *invite* them, and not try to *impress* them, I resolved that afternoon. For I now understood that being hospitable doesn't necessarily mean going all out or having the finest of things. Why, we'd been practicing hospitality all along by opening our hearts and home to Mr. Chang—ungrudgingly—in simple, everyday ways.

I poked a paper flag in each of the hot dogs and passed one to Mr. Chang. "Welcome to our neighborhood! Welcome to America!" I announced with down-home American spirit.

Grandma's grin told me we'd both come to the same conclusion: Puttin' on the dog wouldn't be so complicated next time.

Several years later, Mr. Chang closed his eating establishment. He returned to my grandmother's back door with a set of his restaurant china. "For nurse granddaughter," he explained with his characteristic beaming smile. "In case she ever decides to give up nursing and open a Chinese restaurant."

Roberta Messner

A NEW YEAR'S WISH

How heartily I wish you a happy new year, in all simplicity and truth! Feeling does not depend upon ourselves—only will; and even our will cannot be measured: we cannot take it up like a glove and say, Here it is. You love your son without perpetually worrying yourself to *feel* your love, as you worry yourself to feel your love of God. It is enough that we will to love, and act as best we can accordingly in the spirit of such love. God has no touchy sensitiveness as we have. Let us go straight to Him, and that will do.

Spiritual Letters to Women
François de Salignac de la Moth Fénelon

WHAT'S RED AND WHITE AND KNOWN ALL OVER?

No, the answer to that riddle is *not* the University of Alabama football team, although that wouldn't be a bad guess at all.

Paul (Bear) Bryant became a legend as the football coach at Alabama. In the years which followed his death, stories about this extraordinary man circulated widely. Some were true, some were not, but all of them added to his remarkable mystique.

One such story, one likely to be true, was told by a former player. He was a freshman, and was dressing for his very first game at Tuscaloosa's Bryant-Denney Stadium. On arriving at the locker room, he and the other Bama players found most of their equipment in their lockers, where it was supposed to be, ready to use.

Everything but their game jerseys.

The players said nothing. They simply donned their practice jerseys, which *were* in their lockers, and ran out on the field for their warm-ups. Then they returned to the locker room for a pregame pep talk from their larger-than-life coach.

The Bear remained silent. He strolled around the quiet locker room and made eye contact with each player, one at a time. Then, at the last possible moment, when it was almost time for the players to return to the field, he handed each player a bright crimson jersey.

Words weren't necessary. When those players ran out onto the field, they were sky high, filled with pride. They were part of a winning tradition, and their easily recognized jerseys announced it to the world.

Few of us will ever experience a moment as intense as that one, but we can identify with those players in some small way. It's always nice to be part of a winning tradition and carry a winner's colors.

But the answer to this riddle *isn't* the Crimson Tide. It's the emblem of the Red Cross, a flag which is displayed all over the world, day in and day out, wherever human beings are in need. The Red Cross is *always* there, without fail.

This story is about one small part of that presence—the giving and receiving of blood. And in a sense it isn't even a story. It's a thank you note.

The Judeo-Christian history of human existence on earth begins, of course, with the very first line of the First Book of Moses called Genesis.

> In the beginning, God created
> the heavens and the earth. The earth
> was without form, and void; and darkness
> was on the face of the deep. And the
> Spirit of God was hovering over the
> face of the waters.

> Then God said, "Let there be light";
> and there was light. And God saw the
> light, that it was good; and God divided
> the light from the darkness.
> God called the light Day, and the
> darkness He called Night. So the evening
> and the morning were the first day.

On the second day, God separated the firmament from the waters, calling the firmament Heaven. On the third day he gathered the water to its place and let the dry land appear, which He called Earth. After that, he brought forth vegetation. On the fourth day, he created the two great lights and separated day and night, letting the sun illuminate the day and the moon and stars the night. On the fifth day, he created the fish of the sea, the birds of the air, and the creatures that crawl or walk upon the land.

The Bible tells us that at the end of each day, after he had completed each of these miracles, "God saw that it was good."

On the sixth day, God created man, giving him dominion over the creatures of the sea, the land, and the air. Following *that* accomplishment, God looked at all that he had done and pronounced it "*very* good." A subtle difference, perhaps, but clearly indicative of God's regard for the greatest of his creations.

God knew what he was talking about. The inescapable truth is that man, humankind, is a "very good" creation. Man is a miracle. No doubt about it.

In the first chapter of Genesis, at verse twenty-seven, we are told that when God created man, "male and female He created them." In the second chapter of that book, beginning at verse eighteen, we learn more of the details.

> And the Lord God said, "It is not
> good that the man should be alone; I will
> make him a helper comparable to him."

> And the Lord God caused a deep sleep
> to fall on Adam, and he slept; He took one
> of his ribs, and closed up the flesh
> in its place.

> Then the rib which the Lord God had
> taken from man He made into a woman, and
> He brought her to the man.
> And Adam said: "This is now bone of my bones
> And flesh of my flesh;
> She shall be called Woman,
> Because she was taken out of Man."

Note that only "bones" and "flesh" are specifically mentioned by Adam; there's not a word about blood. So where did Eve's blood come from? Was it Adam's blood? Was it created anew? Rhetorical questions, perhaps, but interesting ones nevertheless. The story continues in chapter four, verse one:

> Now Adam knew Eve his wife, and
> she conceived and bore Cain, and said
> "I have acquired a man from the Lord."

> Then she bore again, this time his
> brother, Abel. Now Abel was a keeper of
> sheep, but Cain was a tiller of the ground.

If all the rest of the creation story wasn't amazing enough, along comes that miracle of miracles, the birth of a baby. Eve gave birth to two sons. First Cain, then Abel.

Consider what happens at the time of conception.

Deep inside the woman, unseen and unfelt, an egg develops, a minuscule collection of tissues *almost* capable of someday becoming a person. Almost, but not quite.

At just the right time, following an ageless instinct, guided only by the natural rhythm of the woman's body, that egg begins a journey. If love's union has been consummated, another miracle may take place, a one-in-a-million miracle called fertilization.

When *that* happens, the egg is fully capable of fulfilling its destiny.

We have no idea what takes place inside the egg at the moment of fertilization. In spite of the efforts of our best scientists and genetic engineers and others who have tried to figure it out for generations, all we really know is that it *happens*, and afterward the egg is different.

How different? Just different enough.

The egg inside the woman's body doesn't stay where it was when it was fertilized. It keeps on moving through its warm, dark world, still following its instinct, still in tune with the woman's natural rhythm. Finally it comes to rest, attaching itself to the wall of the woman's womb.

The egg's cells begin to divide. Very soon, it's large enough and complex enough to need nourishment.

All of this happened inside Eve's body after that very first conception.

When the fertilized egg comes to rest and needs nourishment to survive, another miracle occurs. It is the union of mother and child, a lifeline which will exist, if all goes well, for forty weeks.

That lifeline remained intact inside of Eve until Cain was ready to be born.

The union of Eve and Cain, mother and child, was the *very first* blood transfusion. Eve's blood began flowing into Cain's microscopic veins, carrying nourishment and protection, guarding and sustaining his life.

The giving of blood by one human being to another for the purpose of sustaining life is nothing short of a divinely created miracle. Every human being begins life with a transfusion. No human being can exist without the gift of another person's blood.

In August of 1956, sixteen people stepped inside a Red Cross blood collection center, rolled up their sleeves, and gave the gift of life. All then left the center knowing they had done the right thing. They had *no idea* what would happen to that blood.

Some time later that month, a young man was wheeled into the operating room at a Nashville hospital. By the time the doctors opened him up, he had almost bled to death.

The call went out. The call was answered. Sixteen pints of fresh blood, given by Red Cross volunteers, were ready for just such an emergency.

I was that young man. Almost forty years later, I am still alive.

At Red Cross Blood Services, and at every other volunteer blood donor facility in the world, the bottom line isn't profit, or even breaking even. It isn't statistics such as the number of pints collected or even the number of pints available at any given time. All of that matters, but that's not what it's about.

The bottom line is people. People in crisis who need blood to live. Healthy people who care and are willing to roll up their sleeves.

Those who receive blood when they need it will often never know the identity of their benefactors. Likewise those who donate blood will probably never know the names of those whom they have helped. But I can tell you this—*both* will be happier and better off for the experience. For the recipient, the benefit is obvious. For the donor it is every bit as real. He or she has given a priceless treasure to the one who needs it.

The feeling of satisfaction such a gift can bring its giver is indescribable.

The gratitude felt by recipients like myself, who are alive and well because of the generosity of donors, is indescribable, too. My veins still carry the blood of sixteen different people, men and women whose names I will never know, whose faces I will never see. I thank them from the bottom of my heart.

Richard Speight

TO LOVE GOD MORE

Why, Oh my God, must this mortal structure put so great a separation between my soul and thee? I am surrounded with thy essence, yet I cannot perceive thee: I follow thee, and trace thy footsteps in heaven and earth, yet I cannot overtake thee: thou art before me, and I perceive thee not.

O thou, who, unseen, I love, by what powerful influence dost thou attract my soul? The eye has not seen thee, nor the ear heard, nor has it entered into the heart of man to conceive what thou art; and yet I love thee beyond all that the eye has seen, or my ear heard: beyond all that my heart can comprehend. . . .

My heart cleaves to thee, O Lord, as its only refuge, and finds in thee a secret and constant spring of consolation. I speak to thee with the utmost confidence, and think thy being my greatest happiness. The reflection on thy existence and greatness recreates my spirits, and fills my heart with alacrity: my soul overflows with pleasure: I rejoice, I triumph in thy independent blessedness and absolute dominion. Reign, O my God, for ever, glorious and uncontrolled!

I, a worm of the earth, would join my assent with the infinite orders above, with all the flaming ministers who rejoice in thy kingdom and glory. . . .

I love thee. Thus far I can speak, but all the rest is unutterable; and I must leave the pleasing tale untold, until I can talk in the language of immortality; and then I'll begin the transporting story, which shall never come to an end, but be still and still beginning; for thy beauties, O thou fairest of ten thousand! will still be new, and shall kindle fresh ardor in my soul to all eternity. . . .

Ye angels of God, who behold his face, explain to me the sacred mystery: tell me how this heavenly flame began, unriddle its wondrous generation. Who hath animated this mortal flame with celestial fire, and given a clod of earth this Divine ambition?

Ye flowery varieties of the earth, and ye sparkling glories of the skies, your blandishments are vain, while I pursue an excellence that casts a reproach on all your glory. I would fain close my eyes on all the various and lovely appearances you present, and would open them on a brighter scene. I have desires which nothing visible can gratify, to which no material things are suitable. O when shall I find objects more entirely agreeable to my intellectual faculties! My soul springs forward in pursuit of a distant good, whom I follow by some faint ray of light, which only glimmers by short intervals before me. O when will it disperse the clouds, and break out in full splendor on my soul!

But what will the open vision of the beauties effect, if, while thou art faintly imagined, I love thee with such a sacred fervor! to what blessed heights shall my admiration rise, when I shall behold thee in full protection—when I shall see thee as thou art, exalted in majesty, and complete in beauty! how shall I triumph then in thy glory, and in the privileges of my own being! What ineffable thoughts will rise, to find myself united to the all-sufficient Divinity, by ties which the sons of men have no names to express! . . .

The league of nature shall be broken, and the laws of the mingled elements be canceled; but my relation to the Almighty God shall stand fixed and unchangeable as his own existence: "Nor life, nor death, nor angels, nor principalities, nor powers, nor things present, nor things to come, shall ever separate me from his love."

There are no limits to the prospects of my joy: . . . my bliss is without bounds: O when shall the full possession of it commence!

Elizabeth Rowe

THE UNFRUITFUL TREE

A farmer had a brother in town who was a gardener, and who possessed a magnificent orchard full of the finest fruit trees, so that his skill and his beautiful trees were famous everywhere.

One day the farmer went into town to visit his brother, and was astonished at the rows of trees that grew slender and smooth as wax tapers.

"Look, my brother," said the gardener; "I will give you an apple tree, the best from my garden, and you, and your children, and your children's children shall enjoy it."

Then the gardener called his workmen and ordered them to take up the tree and carry it to his brother's farm. They did so, and the next morning the farmer began to wonder where he should plant it.

"If I plant it on the hill," said he to himself, "the wind might catch it and shake down the delicious fruit before it is ripe; if I plant it close to the road, passers-by will see it and rob me of its luscious apples; but if I plant it too near the door of my house, my servants or the children may pick the fruit."

So, after he had thought the matter over, he planted the tree behind his barn, saying to himself: "Prying thieves will not think to look for it here."

But behold, the tree bore neither fruit nor blossoms the first year nor the second; then the farmer sent for his brother the gardener, and reproached him angrily, saying:—

"You have deceived me, and given me a barren tree instead of a fruitful one. For, behold, this is the third year and still it brings forth nothing but leaves!"

The gardener, when he saw where the tree was planted, laughed and said:—

"You have planted the tree where it is exposed to cold winds, and has neither sun nor warmth. How, then, could you expect flowers and fruit? You have planted the tree with a greedy and suspicious heart; how, then, could you expect to reap a rich and generous harvest?"

Friedrich Adolph Krummacher

THE PERSIAN RULER AND HIS SONS

Once there was a Persian Ruler who lived in a great palace with his three sons. The father had a beautiful pearl which he decided to give to the son which showed himself the most noble. He called the three boys before him and asked each to tell the most noble deed he had performed in the last month.

The eldest said: "Father, as I was traveling in a foreign land, a merchant trusted me with many valuable jewels, and he did not count them. I might easily have kept one or two and they would not have been missed, but I carried those jewels and delivered them all as safely as though they had been my own."

"My son," said the father, "you were honest, and did a noble deed!"

"Father," said the second son, "as I was walking in the country the other day, I saw a child playing by a lake, and while I watched, the child fell in and I saved the child."

"You have done your duty," said the father, "and you too have done a noble deed."

"Father," said the third son, "as I crossed over the mountain the other day, I saw a man who had done me a great wrong sleeping near the edge of a dangerous precipice. I would have walked by without a word, only something within me called me to go back and awake him lest he fall over the precipice and be killed. I did this, knowing all the time that the man would not understand, and that he would be angry with me, as, indeed, he was."

"My son," cried the father, "your deed was the most noble. To do good to an enemy without hope of reward is indeed the most noble of all. The pearl is yours!"

THE CRADLE

A Christmas Story

Joseph's hands worked the rough wood gently and firmly. He held the piece of oak he had selected for the cradle in his rough carpenter's hands, and his thoughts went back over the events of the past few months. Mary, his betrothed, was with child. The knowledge still made him pause in his work. His hands trembled as he recalled how she had told him of the visitation of angels announcing the coming of this child, a son—the son of *God*, to be the Savior of the world! The thoughts staggered the imagination of this simple man, and he fought down the sense of shame and bewilderment that covered him. For days he wrestled with the problem, finally deciding to put her away—gentle, kind and loving Mary who was to be his bride—that she might have this child in private and bring distress and unhappiness to neither his family and friends nor her own. In his country, Nazareth, this was proper; and Joseph, though he loved Mary with his whole heart and soul, was a proper man—well brought up in the traditions and observances of his race. His birthright placed him in the household of David, the beloved shepherd-king of the Israelites. No, he would not show scorn or dismay, but compassion; and he would resolve to make his work his life and never marry.

Then one night, as he lay on his cot sleeping, having made this decision (he remembered her sad eyes and soft voice as he told her of it), the angel Gabriel of the Lord appeared to him. Joseph was perhaps the last man in the world to believe in visions. Sturdy, solid, mature in years, a man with a stubborn streak that Mary knew and had long ago accepted as part of him, he was a good man, but he was not a man of visions. The angel said Mary indeed had been chosen, singled out by Jehovah of all the maids in Judea to bear this child, God's Son; and that he, Joseph, would accept this miracle of miracles and make Mary his wife, following their well laid plans of the weeks and months of their courtship.

The cradle frame was smooth now, and his fingers touched it as if in question. What to use as a design on this cradle (which was the symbol of his acceptance of the angel's instructions of God's will)? He skillfully drew the blade across the wood until there appeared a sunburst radiating from the headpiece. His carving tool seemed inspired, and he worked with no thought of time as the hours passed. Jesus, the expected child, the angel had said, would be the "light of the world." Joseph knew how the earth and crops drew life from the sun. This was indeed a fitting symbol for God's son and for his own amazed and reluctant acceptance of the miracle and God's will. He put from his mind thoughts of a child of his own he longed for and worked instead to finish the cradle, thinking of the coming journey to Bethlehem. All the nations of Jews must go, each to his own birthplace, to be enrolled by the Roman emperor, Caesar Augustus; and Joseph must go to Bethlehem, about five miles from Jerusalem and a good five days journey from Nazareth, with Mary and their belongings, to be listed and taxed as part of the giant Roman empire census. Mary was very near to term, but the order was specific; and they would obey. He had bought a small donkey on which she might ride the weary miles; and as soon as the cradle was finished, they would start. The sun was sinking low in the sky, and its rays cast brilliantly colored hues over the beloved hillside of Galilee that Joseph and his forefathers knew and loved. He began again his gentle rubbing of the satin smooth wood, pausing only to glance in the direction of the animal shelter where the patient, brown-eyed donkey waited and munched his evening straw.

✥   ✥   ✥   ✥

The morning burned brightly above the plains of Nazareth as Joseph led the donkey through the narrow cobble stone streets and lanes to the house where Mary lived. The early morning mist was so thick he could not see clearly; and he was grateful for familiar landmarks, his strong staff and the sure-footed beast beside him. Mary stood in the doorway framed by a strange light, the remains of an early morning fire no doubt. She wore a loose, sturdy white robe and over it, a dark blue wool cloak with a mantle. The climate was warm by day but chilly at night; and they would be traveling over dusty roads, sleeping only a few hours at night with little comfort or privacy. He helped her up on the back of the donkey. She moved slowly, heavy with the weight of the child, but she smiled at him and patted the donkey's rough coat as they started out. The trip was necessary.

It was a command of Caesar himself, and Joseph knew the penalty for ignoring Caesar's commands. He turned the donkey laden with Mary and their provisions to the east and Bethlehem, some sixty-five miles away. As the first rays of the morning sun touched the dew-wet olive trees of Nazareth, they joined the procession of men and women and beasts of burden moving along the road.

The babble of voices was everywhere, children crying, relatives searching for lost ones. Chickens and sheep, brought for food and barter, added their sounds to the noise. The sun rose higher and sweat creased the dust-lined faces of the men and soaked the head-bands of the women. Joseph plodded steadily onward, setting a pace that would keep them ahead of the stragglers and give him time for his thoughts. The cradle was finished. It lay wrapped in oiled cloths in the corner of the house they would occupy on their return. Of all the pieces of furniture he had made, this was the best. Even now his spirits lifted at the remembrance of the beauty of it. His hands were not those of a skilled artisan; but he had poured all his craftsmanship into it and especially the beautifully carved sunburst headpiece, "Fit for a king". The words forced their way into his mind.

Why? Why, out of all the thousands of maids in Judea, had his beloved Mary been chosen of God to bear this "Saviour of the world"? Her gentleness was well known, her sweet smile and kindness to all, young and old, but this holy visitation, this sacred vision, "My soul doth magnify the Lord, and my spirit doth rejoice in God my Saviour. For He hath regarded the low estate of his handmaiden." Mary was saying these words over many times lately, and they were true. The *Lord* himself *had* chosen Mary; and she had accepted this task—to bear this child—the Saviour of the world, the Son of God! Joseph shook his head and strode forward, as if to flee what he did not understand or to hasten the journey. It was then he noticed that many of the other travelers were already camped for the night, drawn in little groups a short piece from the road; their fires lit the evening's glow. It had been a long day. Mary must rest and take nourishment; and the donkey, too, sturdy and faithful with quiet, dark eyes, must have food and drink.

Joseph began preparations for the little group for the night. He chose a slope of land beside the roadway close to the other travelers but far away enough to give Mary privacy. He made a bed for Mary before the small fire. Tired, they ate in silence, as the first stars appeared, Mary's face was thoughtful and resigned. They lay down, grateful for peace and the end of this first day of the journey.

Joseph was an early riser by habit, but he hated to awaken Mary. He spent some time with the little donkey, and he was happy to see Mary's glad smile. Her eyes lighted; and she said, half reprovingly, as she prepared their meager breakfast, "Joseph, you are such a good man! To care for this little donkey while I slept! Lazy me. You must call me at first light. We have a long journey, and I must help." She winced a bit as she felt the child move within her. Goodness, how strong he was! Seated once more on the donkey, she remembered the unusual events of the past weeks. The dust rose in clouds and the voices faded in the distance as Mary saw again the angel who had foretold the coming of this special child. Truly her people had waited many years in physical and spiritual bondage for a Messiah. Could it be that the time had arrived for this long-awaited king? Mary was a simple country girl, and she knew that the life within her moved and kicked at times as if to be set free. She placed her hands over her rounded belly and pressed down gently, singing in her soft, sweet voice, a lullaby to her unborn son.

The days and nights passed slowly. As they neared Bethlehem, Mary grew more tired, dark circles appeared around her eyes, and she spoke little. Joseph hoped to cheer her by telling her of the cradle he had made for their child; but as the people pressed forward, eager to get the journey over and find suitable lodgings, the little group fell behind; and it was all Joseph could do to guide the tired donkey and keep the rising dust from choking him each time he spoke. He found his way to Mary's side and offered her water from a goatskin bag. She took it gratefully and paused to pour a bit of the cool water on her hands and press them to her hot, tired face. "I have a surprise," Joseph began, "something I made for the child." She smiled slightly and then swayed as if to fall. He steadied her and held his peace. There would be time for telling of the cradle when they were safe in lodgings in Bethlehem, and Mary was taken care of by a mid-wife, for surely the time was near. He turned suddenly and slapped the little donkey's bottom. "Get on with you, faithful one. Get on, and hurry as fast as your little hoofs can go. For the child will come soon and your mistress must have shelter and care." The donkey obeyed as if he understood, and as the sun sank below the rims of the hills, the lights of the town of Bethlehem loomed in the distance.

And high above, newly risen in the east, was a star of such beauty and light, Joseph was forced to shade his eyes to look upon it.

❋　❋　❋

Bethlehem was a mad house. Tired people, animals and uniformed Roman soldiers were everywhere. The quiet city Joseph remembered was a sweating, heaving mass of humans, all intent on finding lodgings or, if they were so lucky, in meeting old friends, exchanging gossip and buying or bartering livestock or goods.

Leading the donkey, Joseph made his way through the crowded streets of Bethlehem. Everything had changed it seemed. The city was not large; but the milling crowds and coming darkness gave it such an unreal atmosphere, he was lost for a moment. He went first to the house of a distant relative; but though he and Mary were greeted warmly, the man had only a small house, and his sons and daughters more than filled it. Mary was growing more and more weary; and Joseph, confused and tired, thought of the comfortable room in Nazareth and the beautiful cradle ready to receive the child. They knocked on many doors; inns, hostelries and lodgings of all sorts, but there was no place to be found. No place at all, even though night had come and Mary was very tired. The donkey was steady and patient, but Joseph grew more and more concerned as the hours stretched on. Finally, at the end of the lane, there were lights and the sound of laughter—an inn! Joseph's heart leapt for joy. Here at last, there would be a place. He knocked quickly and stated his needs, only to be met with the same story, "no room". He gazed beyond the doorway at the crowd, the food and laughter, and began for the first time to doubt that there was a God. Surely, if this child Mary carried was God's son, was there no place to be provided for his birth? Mary's beseeching look was not lost on the innkeeper's wife nor was the evident tiredness of the little donkey. A spark of sympathy crept into her eyes, and she motioned her burly husband aside. "The stable," she said, "the stable is large enough, too, for these." He looked dubiously at the little trio and then at her face. For the first time in a long time, he saw pleading there. "Yes," he thought, "there *was* room but little comfort, warmth or food. Still, the man was exhausted, the woman near child and the donkey barely able to stand." He nodded, and they pointed to the stable far at the end of the lane. It was easy to see; because it seemed flooded with light from the strange, beautiful star Joseph had seen. After they found a place among the beasts, Mary looked up through the rafters and saw the huge star, so close it seemed to almost hang suspended above them. A song, soft and clear, came from nowhere; and she felt the child move to enter the world. No cry rose to her lips until the innkeeper's wife, with Joseph, appeared from nowhere. "Cry my pretty one," she said, "your lips will be red with blood." She pressed a cool cloth to Mary's head and bent to bring the child into the world. A strapping man-child but few tears, like his mother. One swat, and he was placed at her breast. The innkeeper brought a pot of thin gruel, and Mary sipped it gratefully. Joseph watched in alternating amazement and adoration. He had witnessed birth before but not like this. They swaddled the tiny, dark-haired babe in cloths and looked about for a bed. Joseph thought of the cradle, carved and beautiful, waiting in Nazareth. Suddenly, a light illuminated the stable and settled on the manger-bed, old and worn and filled with fresh hay for the animals. It was to be the cradle of the King.

And Joseph bowed before the knowledge that Jehovah is God, and God is God and Christ is God's son; and they laid him in a manger.

And suddenly, angel music filled the air; and the sounds of, "Glory to God in the highest, and on earth Peace to men of good will", could he heard echoing and re-echoing over the Bethlehem plain. And Joseph's heart sang with the angels, seeing the tender scene of Mary and the sweet babe in the manger, the Cradle of God.

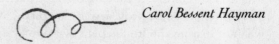

Carol Bessent Hayman

PRUDENCE

Prudence is thinking ahead and planning to do the right or the best thing in any happening. If we are prudent, we pursue the wisdom of the ages, we take counsel from others, we listen for God's voice, we plan before we act. Thomas Aquinas called prudence the "rudder virtue." The prudent person sails straight in any of life's storms, while an imprudent person is like a ship without a rudder, drifting aimlessly in a sea of choices.

The wisdom of the prudent is to give thought to their ways, but the folly of fools is deception.

Proverbs 14:8 NIV

Awake My Soul

Awake, my soul, and with the sun
Thy daily stage of duty run;
Shake off dull sloth, and joyful rise
To pay thy morning sacrifice!

In conversation be sincere:
Keep conscience as the noon-tide clear;
Think how all-seeing God thy ways
And all thy secret thought surveys.

Lord, I my vows to thee renew;
Disperse my sins as morning dew;
Guard my first springs of thought and will,
And with thyself my spirit fill.

Direct, control, suggest this day
All I design to do or say,
That all my powers, with all their might,
In thy sole glory may unite.

Thomas Ken
1637–1711

COME WHAT MAY, WE CAN TRUST GOD

Search Institute in Minneapolis, Minnesota, recently conducted a fascinating research project in which they surveyed more than 11,000 people from 561 different Protestant congregations. One question they asked was this: What constitutes mature faith? What are the marks of genuine spiritual maturity?

From that study, they concluded that spiritually mature people always seem to exhibit eight very special qualities:

1. They trust in God's saving grace, and they believe firmly in the humanity and divinity of Jesus.

2. They feel good about themselves; they experience a sense of personal well-being, security, and peace.

3. They integrate faith and life, seeing work, family, social relationships, and political choices as part of one's religious life.

4. They seek spiritual growth through study, reflection, prayer, and discussion with others.

5. They seek to be part of a community of believers in which people give witness to their faith, and support and nourish one another.

6. They hold life-affirming values, including commitment to racial and gender equality, affirmation of cultural and religious diversity, and a personal sense of responsibility for the welfare of others.

7. They advocate social and global change to bring about greater peace and justice.

8. They serve humanity consistently and passionately, through acts of love and justice.

It's significant to note that five of these eight characteristics involve seeing Christ in our neighbors and knowing that in serving them, we are serving him. Remember how Jesus said it in Matthew 25:40: "Truly I tell you just as you did it to one of the least of these . . . you did it to me."

It's also interesting to note how closely these Search Institute marks of mature faith resemble the Beatitudes. Matthew 5 is not a list of clever proverbs or a compilation of unrelated, independent sayings. Rather, what we have in the Beatitudes is a step-by-step outline of the faith pilgrimage, a chronological description of the way the spiritual life unfolds, how it develops and matures:

1. First, we are poor in spirit—that is, we humbly recognize how much we need God.

2. Second, we mourn our sins.

3. Third, in meekness, we offer ourselves unconditionally as God's servants; we commit our lives totally to God.

4. Next, we want to learn the faith, to grow spiritually; we hunger and thirst for righteousness.

5. Then we go out into the world to live the faith in the spirit of mercy . . .

6. . . . and the spirit of genuineness, being authentic—not being hypocritical, but pure in heart.

7. Finally, we come to the height of spiritual maturity. In the spirit of God, we become peacemakers, reconcilers.

8. Then Jesus adds a P.S.: "Oh, by the way," he says, "if you do these things—if you live the Beatitudes out there in the day-to-day world—you may well be persecuted. People may turn against you. They may give you a hard time, but don't be afraid, because I am with you. I will protect you. I will see you through."

James W. Moore

THE NAIL

A merchant had done good business at the fair; he had sold his wares, and filled his bag with gold and silver. Then he set out at once on his journey home, for he wished to be in his own house before night.

At noon he rested in a town. When he wanted to go on, the stable-boy brought his horse, saying: "A nail is wanting, sir, in the shoe of his left hind foot."

"Let it be wanting," answered the merchant; "the shoe will stay on for the six miles I have still to go. I am in a hurry."

In the afternoon he got down at an inn and had his horse fed. The stable-boy came into the room to him and said: "Sir, a shoe is wanting from horse's left hind foot. Shall I take him to the blacksmith?"

"Let it still be wanting," said the man; "the horse can very well hold out for a couple of miles more. I am in a hurry."

So the merchant rode forth, but before long the horse began to limp. He had not limped long before he began to stumble, and he had not stumbled long before he fell down and broke his leg. The merchant had to leave the horse where he fell, and unstrap the bag, take it on his back, and go home on foot.

"That unlucky nail," said he to himself, "has made all this trouble."

The Brothers Grimm (Translated)

PLANTING AN ORCHARD

Once there was a man who wanted to plant an orchard of apple trees. He sent to a nursery for some young plants, and when they came all wrapped up in a good bundle, he thought of what fine trees he was going to have, and the beautiful apples they would bear.

The bundle came just about the time the man was starting to town on some business. So he sent off at once for a man who knew how to plant trees, and said to him, "Here are my young apple trees, and I want you to plant them for me. I shall be gone all day," and he showed the man where to plant them.

When he came back later in the afternoon the man had planted only six trees. The owner was surprised and said, "It seems to me you work very slowly."

The man replied, "Yes, but I do my work thoroughly. You see I dug great holes so that the roots of the young trees might not be broken or cramped; then I hauled rich earth from the woods, and mixed it well with the top soil; then I packed the earth carefully around the roots so that it would be firm; and then I watered each plant until it was thoroughly soaked. All that takes time, and one must not be in a hurry about planting a tree if he expects it to live and flourish."

"That sounds very fine," said the owner, "but it is too slow a way for me. I could have planted five times as many in a day. You take too much trouble." So he dismissed the man and the next day he planted his orchard in his own way.

He dug the holes just large enough to hold the roots by twisting them together, and many of the rootlets were broken or injured as they were forced into place; he did not get the soft rich earth from the woods, nor was he careful in packing the dirt around the roots, and then he did not fill the holes with water.

"Now, see there," he said to himself, "I have planted a whole orchard in one day."

But see what happened! The trees the owner planted so carelessly lived for a while, and put out a few leaves. They bore some little apples, and then the owner cut them down. But the six trees the other man planted grew up strong and healthy. In a few years they were well shaped and tall and began to bear quantities of the most beautiful apples. When the owner was an old man they still were standing, and everybody would say, "What wonderful apple trees! What splendid fruit!"

But the old man knew he could have had a whole orchard like that if he had planted them all as the six were planted.

Lawton B. Evans

GOD IS ABLE

One of the great problems that faces us today is despair. When we come upon some situation which seems too much for us, the real temptation is to lose heart. When we are confronted with obstacles which seem insurmountable, we too often retreat acknowledging defeat. When we look at what ought to be done and then why it seems impossible to do it, we throw up our hands and say "not now!"

But most of the time when we feel defeated and overcome with despair, we forget that that there are resources other than our own, that God is able to see us through.

It is interesting to note that there is a recurring theme in our Bible which says: *God is able*. In Jude 24 the writer is apparently speaking to those who face temptations when he writes: "Unto him that is able to keep you from falling." Paul puts it like this in Romans 14:4: "God is able to make him stand."

When we are hesitant, there is this confident note sounded by Paul in his Letter to the Philippians: "Able even to subdue all things unto himself" (3:21). When we are tempted to confine God within the boundaries of our own inadequate calculations and feel that he is limited within our cramping expectations, let us listen to these words from Ephesians 3:20: "Now unto him that is able to do exceeding abundantly above all that we ask or think."

And in II Corinthians 9:8 Paul continues to affirm the power of God when he writes: "God is able to make all grace abound toward you; that ye, always having all sufficiency in all things, may abound to every good work." Indeed our God is *able*. Let us see how we forget this in our affairs.

It is so easy for us to assign God a *secondary role in the world scene*. We are prone to add up the number of bombers and atomic carriers other countries have compared to our own output. We figure the number of men in arms, the size of the navy, the types of guns being produced, as compared to that of our own and of our friends. We give great thought to the location of airfields, and the control of waterways.

Now to be sure, realism does force our leaders to so consider. We must give thought to the resources at hand and their availability for the future. It would be suicidal to blindly go through life and not give heed to what human hands can do.

But what I'm concerned about is that we not omit God in our planning, that we remember God is alive and active in our affairs, that God still is in command of the world, that in his possession are forces which can change God's hearts and alter the tides of time. Let us not forget that this is God's world and it will be run according to God's plan or it will not run.

History bears evidence to the fact that the moral laws of God will prevail, that in the end the nation or people that honor those laws are the ones which will stand.

Yes, as Paul said, God "is able even to subdue all things unto himself." This is a tonic which can give us hope for times like these.

God is able, not only on the world scene, *but also in our personal lives*. When we face despair, when we meet obstacles, to be sure we must take into account the physical resources at hand. It is right that we explore to the fullest the brains given us and the talents available. But after we have done this, let's not rule God out.

"Unto him that is able to keep you from falling"—he becomes our hope in time of temptation. When we are prone to falter along the way, remember "God is able to make us stand."

Maybe some of you feel that your life is a failure. You are in despair. Sin has made you sick. You no longer gain joy out of living. Life has no meaning. You are ready to throw in the towel. Or maybe you have a loved one whose life has been broken by evil living. You are beginning to feel that there is no hope for him. Your home is almost broken because of sinful ways.

Or perchance some of you feel that life has crowded you in a corner and you see no way out—only a dead-end street. Tragedy has come your way. It may be through broken health. It may be financial distress. It may be an aching sorrow. It may be a physical limitation.

Well, here is hope for you. Our God "is able to do exceeding abundantly above all that we ask or think." God is able to take what seems to be a hopeless, helpless broken person and make that person whole again. He can take a person who does not want to live and make that person fall in love with life again.

Paul, the great apostle, a man of dynamic action and creative ability, once said, "For we were so utterly, unbearably crushed that we despaired of life itself" (2 Corinthians 1:8 RSV), and yet he said, "God is able to make him stand," and in that faith he became the world's greatest missionary.

There is no greater need in our time than that of counting on God. As William Carey has well phrased it: "Expect great things from God. Attempt great things for God."

To be sure God expects us to use to the fullest all the gifts and powers with which we are endowed, to be wise as our wisdom will let us be; but he also expects us to leave some things to him, to live by faith in his promises. And soon we discover that as Ralph W. Sockman says, "the more we lean on God, the more we stand on our own feet. The more we hold to him, the more we find personal sufficiency."

Wallace Fridy

A DINNER OF TONGUES

Aesop was the servant of a philosopher named Xanthus. One day his master being desirous of entertaining some of his friends to dinner, he ordered him to provide the best things he could find in the market. Aesop thereupon made a large provision of tongues, which he desired the cook to serve up with different sauces. When dinner came, the first and second courses, the side dishes, and the removes, were all tongues.

"Did I not order you," said Xanthus, in a violent passion, "to buy the best victuals which the market afforded?"

"And have I not obeyed your orders?" said Aesop. "Is there any thing better than tongues? Is not the tongue the bond of civil society, the key of science, and the organ of truth and reason? It is by means of the tongue cities are built, and governments established and administered; with it men instruct, persuade, and preside in assemblies; it is the instrument with which we acquit ourselves of the chief of four duties, the praising and adoring of the Deity."

"Well then," replied Xanthus, "go to market tomorrow and buy me the worst things you can find. This same company shall dine with me, and I have a mind to change my entertainment."

When Xanthus assembled his friends the next day, he was astonished to find that Aesop had provided nothing but the very same dishes.

"Did I not tell you," said Xanthus, "to provide the worst things for this day's feast? How comes it, then, that you have placed before us the same kind of food, which only yesterday you declared to be the very best?"

Aesop, not, at all abashed, replied: "The tongue is the worst thing in the world as well as the best; for it is the instrument of all strife and contention, the fomenter of lawsuits, the source of division and war, the organ of error, of calumny, of falsehood, and even of profanity."

The conduct of Aesop, in this affair, my young friends, is quite instructive. For it is certainly true, that the tongue, according to circumstances, may be, and is the best or the worst thing in the world. Rightly used, it is the fittest organ of wisdom, wrongly used, it becomes the foulest medium of folly and wickedness.

"For," says the Bible, "every kind of beasts, and of birds, and of serpents, and of things in the sea, is tamed, and hath been tamed of mankind; but the tongue can no man tame; it is an unruly evil, full of deadly poison. Therewith bless we God, even the Father; and therewith curse we men, which are made after the similitude of God. Out of the same mouth proceedeth blessing and cursing. My brethren, these things ought not to be."

The New School Reader, 1864

TAMING THE TONGUE

Not many of you should become teachers, my brothers and sisters, for you know that we who teach will be judged with greater strictness. For all of us make many mistakes. Anyone who makes no mistakes in speaking is perfect, able to keep the whole body in check with a bridle. If we put bits into the mouths of horses to make them obey us, we guide their whole bodies. Or look at ships: though they are so large that it takes strong winds to drive them, yet they are guided by a very small rudder wherever the will of the pilot directs. So also the tongue is a small member, yet it boasts of great exploits.

How great a forest is set ablaze by a small fire! And the tongue is a fire. The tongue is placed among our members as a world of iniquity; it stains the whole body, sets on fire the cycle of nature, and is itself set on fire by hell. For every species of beast and bird, of reptile and sea creature, can be tamed and has been tamed by the human species, but no one can tame the tongue—a restless evil, full of deadly poison. With it we bless the Lord and Father, and with it we curse those who are made in the likeness of God. From the same mouth come blessing and cursing. My brothers and sisters, this ought not to be so. Does a spring pour forth from the same opening both fresh and brackish water? Can a fig tree, my brothers and sisters, yield olives, or a grapevine figs? No more can salt water yield fresh.

Who is wise and understanding among you? Show by your good life that your works are done with gentleness born of wisdom. But if you have bitter envy and selfish ambition in your hearts, do not be boastful and false to the truth. Such wisdom does not come down from above, but is earthly, unspiritual, devilish. For where there is envy and selfish ambition, there will also be disorder and wickedness of every kind. But the wisdom from above is first pure, then peaceable, gentle, willing to yield, full of mercy and good fruits, without a trace of partiality or hypocrisy. And a harvest of righteousness is sown in peace for those who make peace.

James 3 NRSV

SO BE ON YOUR GUARD

Mark 13 emphasizes one command: Be alert, watch! No less than five verses repeat the exhortation to be prepared for the turmoil and deceptions which lie ahead.

I can still hear Doc Hatcher, the father of a fellow Scout, telling our troop as we were leaving for camp: "Have a good time; be a good Scout. Be prepared."

His advice has stayed with me for more than twenty-five years, and I have followed it with varying degrees of success.

From the viewpoint of faith, our lives may not have been graced with a "good time"; most surely, our "good Scout" days have been more than equaled by our "bad Scout" days! And who is bold enough to say they've always been prepared? Few of us are consistent in following commands. Most advice received is advice eventually forgotten.

Faith, finally, is trusting that Someone Else is better prepared than we for what lies ahead.

Barry Culbertson

THE DAY AND HOUR UNKNOWN

"No one knows about that day or hour, not even the angels in heaven, nor the Son, but only the Father. Be on guard! Be alert! You do not know when that time will come. It's like a man going away: He leaves his house in charge of his servants, each with his assigned task, and tells the one at the door to keep watch.

"Therefore keep watch because you do not know when the owner of the house will come back—whether in the evening, or at midnight, or when the rooster crows, or at dawn. If he comes suddenly, do not let him find you sleeping. What I say to you, I say to everyone: 'Watch!' "

Mark 13:32-37 NIV

ON SILENCE AND RECOLLECTION

I think, Madame, that you should try hard to learn to practice silence, so far as general courtesy will admit of. Silence promotes the Presence of God, avoids many harsh or proud words, and suppresses many dangers in the way of ridiculing or rashly judging our neighbors. Silence humbles the mind, and detaches it from the world; it would create a kind of solitude in the heart like that you court; it would supply much that you need under present difficulties. If you retrenched all useless talk, you would have many available moments even amid the inevitable claims of society. You wish for freedom for prayer; while God, Who knows what you need better than you do, surrounds you with restraints and hampering claims. The hindrances which beset you in the order of God's Providence will profit you more than any possible self-delectation in devotion. You know very well that retirement is not essential to the love of God. When He gives you time, you must take it and use it; but meanwhile abide patiently, satisfied that whatever He allots you is best. Lift up your heart to Him continually, without making any outward sign; only talk when it is necessary, and bear quietly with what crosses you. As you grow in the faith, God will treat you accordingly. You stand more in need of mortification than of light. The only thing I dread for you is dissipation; but you may remedy even that by silence. If you are stedfast in keeping silence when it is not necessary to speak, God will preserve you from evil when it is right for you to talk.

If you are unable to secure much time to yourself, be all the more careful about stray moments. Even a few minutes gleaned faithfully amid engagements will be more profitable in God's Sight than whole hours given up to Him at freer seasons. Moreover, many brief spaces of time through the day will amount to something considerable at last. Possibly you yourself may find the advantage of such frequent recollection in God's Presence more than in a regular definite period allotted to devotion.

Your lot, Madame, is to love, to be silent, and to sacrifice your inclinations, in order to fulfill the Will of God by molding yourself to that of others. Happy indeed you are thus to bear a cross laid on you by God's Own Hands in the order of His Providence. The penitential work we choose, or even accept at the hands of others, does not so stifle, self-love as that which God assigns us from day to day. In it we find nothing to foster self, and, coming as it does directly from His Merciful Providence, it brings with it grace sufficient for all our needs. All we have to do is to give ourselves up to God day by day, without looking further; He will carry us in His Arms as a loving mother carries her child. Let us believe, hope, love, with a child's simplicity, in every need looking with affection and trust to our Heavenly Father. He has said in His Own Word, "Can a woman forget her sucking child? . . . Yea, she may forget, yet will I not forget thee."

François de Salignac de la Moth Fénelon

PRACTICE SPIRITUAL DISCIPLINE

Christians who are not instructed in the fundamentals of Christianity are not likely to mature into solid saints. I sincerely believe a poor foundation is the reason many are not steadfast today. Dear saint, do not be too proud to go back and learn the basic precepts of the Gospel if you have not yet mastered them. Too many are more concerned about their reputation than their salvation.

Wait on the ministry of the Word. The apostle cautioned the Hebrew Christians nor to neglect church attendance (Hebrews 10:25). If you say you want to know God's truth, but neglect to go where the Word is preached, you are as insincere as the man who says he wants to watch the sun set but will not bother to turn his chair toward the west.

To know God, you must come to where He has appointed you to learn. If there is a church, go. If there is none, study your Bible diligently and wait on the ministry of the Spirit at home. You can trust your heavenly Father to use extraordinary measures to honor your demand for spiritual food. He is like a father who, if there is no school in town, teaches his child at home and turns him into an excellent scholar. God, Paul tells us, "maketh manifest the savor of his knowledge by us in every place" (2 Corinthians 2:14).

God's Word is filled with good things for your soul. He wants you to have them all, so see to it that you are a wakeful and attentive student. Strive to be like Lydia, who "attended unto the things which were spoken by Paul" (Acts 16:14). When you go to church, try to fix your quicksilver mind and set yourself to hear the sermon. Above all, make sure your heart is consumed with love for God, and your will is in submission to His desires. The mind goes on the will's errand; we spend our thoughts on what our hearts propose.

William Gurnall

PASTOR NOODLE'S LIGHT

Jonathan and Thomas were constantly arguing. Whenever they saw each other, which was often because they were next door neighbours, they found something rude to say. One day, Jonathan would criticise Thomas for allowing his cattle to lean over the fence and eat grass from Jonathan's field. The next day Thomas would be angry with Jonathan because nettles from Jonathan's land were spreading on to Thomas's land. Their two wives were close friends, and they longed for Jonathan and Thomas to be friends.

Eventually one winter, the two long suffering women decided that they could stand it no longer. "Christmas will soon be here," they said to their husbands. "It's supposed to be the season of peace and goodwill. Surely you can learn to be at peace with each other and stop arguing."

But the very next day, Thomas accused Jonathan of shoveling snow on to his land—and a fierce argument arose.

So their wives went to Pastor Noodle to see if he could find an answer.

Pastor Noodle thought for a few moments, stroking his long white beard. Finally he spoke. "I think I have an answer. Leave it to me." Pastor Noodle went immediately to see Jonathan and Thomas, calling them together outside their houses.

"I want you to enter a competition with me on Christmas Eve," Pastor Noodle began. "It will provide entertainment for the whole village. The competition is this. We will divide the barn outside the vicarage into three equal parts. Between dawn and dusk, we will see which of us can fill our part the fullest, using anything we like. If either of you win, you can take all the fruit and vegetables that grow in the garden over the next year. If I win, you must promise never to argue again, and instead learn to be friends."

Jonathan and Thomas thought they had nothing to lose, so they agreed to the competition. At dawn on Christmas Eve, the whole village gathered around the barn.

As soon as the sun was visible above the eastern horizon, Jonathan and Thomas began rushing around the village collecting anything they could find to fill their parts of the barn—bales of straw, old buckets, sacks of potatoes, and whatever else they could carry.

But Pastor Noodle was nowhere to be seen.

At lunch time, Jonathan and Thomas were still busy. And Pastor Noodle was still nowhere to be seen. A few hours later, as the sun began to set below the western horizon, Jonathan and Thomas had both filled their parts of the barn almost to the roof. But Pastor Noodle's part was still completely empty.

Finally, as the last rays of sun were fading, Pastor Noodle came out of his house, carrying an unlit candle. He walked into the barn and placed the candle in the middle. He spoke the verse from the opening chapter of John's Gospel: "The light of Christ shines in the darkness, and the darkness cannot overcome it." Then he knelt down and lit the candle.

In the darkness of Christmas Eve, its light filled the whole barn, shining right up into the rafters of the roof. A great cheer arose as everyone realized that Pastor Noodle had won the competition. Jonathan and Thomas stepped forward. Standing over the candle, they shook hands. And from that Christmas onwards, they were the firmest of friends.

Robert Van De Weyer

THE MAN ON THE CHIMNEY

Once upon a time, some workmen were repairing the tall chimney of a factory. It was so tall that no ladder could reach its top, so the men went up and down on a rope. The rope passed through a pulley which was firmly fixed to the top of the chimney.

At last the work was ended. The workmen came down quickly, glad to be safe on the ground once more.

When the next to the last man reached the ground, by mistake he pulled the rope from the pulley. Then he looked back and saw another man standing alone on the chimney.

"Oh! What have I done!" he cried. "Poor fellow, what will become of him? He cannot get down! He will die!"

The workmen were so alarmed that they could think of no way to help their comrade. They stood helpless, looking first at the coil of rope at their feet and then at their friend high in the air.

"He will starve if he stays there, and he will be killed if he tries to climb down," they said sadly.

Just then the wife of the man appeared. She did not cry, scold, or fret. Instead, she said to herself, "What can I do to save him? There must be some way."

Soon a bright idea came to her, and she shouted to her husband:—

"John! John! Unravel your stocking! Begin at the toe!"

John understood at once. He took off the coarse yarn stocking that she had knit for him, cut off the toe, and began to unravel the yarn.

When he had pulled out a long piece, he tied the end around a small piece of brick. This he very carefully let down to the ground.

How eagerly the men below seized upon it. They fastened the yarn to a ball of twine which John's wife had brought. Then they shouted:—

"Pull up the yarn till you get the twine."

Soon John called to them:—

"I have it."

They next fastened the twine to a heavy rope and shouted:—

"Pull up the twine till you get the rope."

"All right," said John, and in a very few minutes he held the stout rope in his hand. With its aid, he let himself safely down to the ground. How they all cheered as his foot touched the earth!

Do you think he left the remnant of his stocking on the chimney-top? No, indeed. He brought it down, buttoned under his coat. It was a precious keepsake. He often showed it to his children, as he told them the wonderful story of how his life had been saved by their mother.

Fanny E. Coe

KNOWLEDGE AND WISDOM

Do your best to present yourself to God as one approved, a workman who does not need to be ashamed and who correctly handles the word of truth.

Continue in what you have learned and have become convinced of, because you know those from whom you learned it, and how from infancy you have known the holy Scriptures, which are able to make you wise for salvation through faith in Christ Jesus.

All Scripture is God-breathed and is useful for teaching, rebuking, correcting and training in righteousness, so that the man of God may be thoroughly equipped for every good work.

Preach the Word; be prepared in season and out of season; correct, rebuke and encourage—with great patience and careful instruction.

I have hidden your word in my heart that I might not sin against you.

Your word, O Lord is eternal; it stands firm in the heavens.

Your word is a lamp to my feet and a light to my path.

Your statutes are wonderful; therefore I obey them.

The entrance of your words give light; it gives understanding to the simple.

Direct my footsteps according to your word; let no sin rule over me.

Your promises have been thoroughly tested, and your servant loves them.

Hear my voice in accordance with your love; renew my life, O Lord, according to your laws.

2 Timothy 2:15; 3:14-17; 4:2
Psalm 119:11, 89, 105, 129, 130, 133, 140, 149 NIV

THE CHOICE OF HERCULES

Long, long ago, when the world was young, there were many deeds waiting to be wrought by daring heroes. It was then that the mighty Hercules, who was yet a lad, felt an exceeding great and strong desire to go out into the wide world to seek his fortune.

One day, while wandering alone and thoughtful, he came to a place where two paths met. And sitting down he gravely considered which he should follow.

One path led over flowery meadows toward the darkening distance; the other, passing over rough stones and rugged, brown furrows, lost itself in the glowing sunset.

And as Hercules gazed into the distance, he saw two stately maidens coming toward him.

The first was tall and graceful, and wrapped round in a snow-white mantle. Her countenance was calm and beautiful. With gracious mien and modest glance she drew near the lad.

The other maiden made haste to outrun the first. She, too, was tall, but seemed taller than she really was. She, too, was beautiful, but her glance was bold. As she ran, a rosy garment like a cloud floated about her form, and she kept looking at her own round arms and shapely hands, and ever and anon she seemed to gaze admiringly at her shadow as it moved along the ground. And this fair one did outstrip the first maiden, and rushing forward held out her white hands to the lad, exclaiming: —

"I see thou art hesitating, O Hercules, by what path to seek thy fortune. Follow me along this flowery way, and I will make it a delightful and easy road. Thou shalt taste to the full of every kind of pleasure. No shadow of annoyance shall ever touch thee, nor strain nor stress of war and state disturb thy peace. Instead thou shalt tread upon carpets soft as velvet, and sit at golden tables, or recline upon silken couches. The fairest of maidens shall attend thee, music and perfume shall lull thy senses, and all that is delightful to eat and drink shall be placed before thee. Never shalt thou labor, but always live in joy and ease. Oh, come! I give my followers liberty and delight!"

And as she spoke the maiden stretched forth her arms, and the tones of her voice were sweet and caressing.

"What, O maiden," asked Hercules, "is thy name?"

"My friends," said she, "call me Happiness, but mine enemies name me Vice."

Even as she spoke, the white-robed maiden, who had drawn near, glided forward, and addressed the lad in gracious tones and with words stately and winning:—

"O beloved youth, who wouldst wander forth in search of Life, I too, would plead with thee! I, Virtue, have watched and tended thee from a child. I know the fond care thy parents have bestowed to train thee for a hero's part. Direct now thy steps along yon rugged path that leads to my dwelling. Honorable and noble mayest thou become through thy illustrious deeds.

"I will not seduce thee by promises of vain delights; instead will I recount to thee the things that really are. Lasting fame and true nobility come not to mortals save through pain and labor. If thou, O Hercules, seekest the gracious gifts of Heaven, thou must remain constant in prayer; if thou wouldst be beloved of thy friends, thou must serve thy friends; if thou desirest to be honored of the people thou must benefit the people; if thou art anxious to reap the fruits of the earth, thou must till the earth with labor; and if thou wishest to be strong in body and accomplish heroic deeds, thou must teach thy body to obey thy mind. Yea, all this and more also must thou do."

"Seest thou not, O Hercules," cried Vice, "over how difficult and tedious a road this Virtue would drive thee? I, instead, will conduct thy steps by a short and easy path to perfect Happiness."

"Wretched being!" answered Virtue, "wouldst thou deceive this lad! What lasting Happiness hast thou to offer! Thou pamperest thy followers with riches; thou deludest them with idleness; thou surfeitest them with luxury; thou enfeeblest them with softness. In youth they grow slothful in body and weak in mind. They live without labor and wax fat. They come to a wretched old age, dissatisfied, and ashamed, and oppressed by the memory of their ill deeds; and, having run their course, they lay themselves down in melancholy death and their name is remembered no more.

"But those fortunate youths who follow me receive other counsel. I am the companion of virtuous men. Always I am welcome in the homes of artisans and in the cottages of tillers of the soil. I am the guardian of industrious households, and the rewarder of generous masters and faithful servants. I am the promoter of the labors of peace. No honorable deed is accomplished without me.

"My friends have sweet repose and the untroubled enjoyment of the fruits of their efforts. They remember their deeds with an easy conscience and contentment, and are beloved of their friends and honored by their country. And when they have run their course, and death overtakes them, their names are celebrated in song and praise, and they live in the hearts of their grateful countrymen.

"Come, then, O Hercules, thou son of noble parents, come, follow thou me, and by thy worthy and illustrious deeds secure for thyself exalted Happiness."

She ceased, and Hercules, withdrawing his gaze from the face of Vice, arose from his place, and followed Virtue along the rugged, brown path of Labor.

Xenophon (Adapted)

JUSTICE

J ustice is concerned with rights and with the duties that correspond to those rights. As Christians we are concerned that everyone receive his or her due; we believe in contributing out of our resources and gifts to the common good of all; we cannot be indifferent to issues of justice; instead we believe it is our duty to get involved when others are victimized by unfair practices.

What does the Lord require of you but to do justice and to love kindness and to walk humbly with your God?

Micah 6:8 NRSV

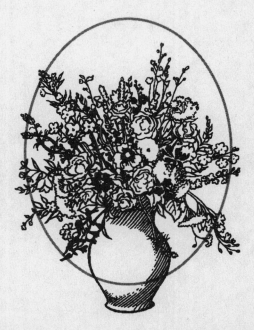

A GREAT LIGHT

The people that walked in darkness have seen a great light: they that dwell in the land of the shadow of death, upon them hath the light shined.

Thou hast multiplied the nation, and not increased the joy: they joy before thee according to the joy in harvest, and as men rejoice when they divide the spoil.

For thou hast broken the yoke of his burden, and the staff of his shoulder, the rod of his oppressor, as in the day of Midian.

For every battle of the warrior is with confused noise, and garments rolled in blood; but this shall be with burning and fuel of fire.

For unto us a child is born, unto a son is given: and the government shall be upon his shoulder: and his name shall be called Wonderful, Counsellor, The mighty God, The everlasting Father, The Prince of Peace.

Of the increase of his government and peace there shall be no end, upon the throne of David, and upon his kingdom, to order it, and to establish it with judgment and with justice from henceforth even for ever. The zeal of the Lord of hosts will perform this.

Isaiah 9:2-7 KJV

LET YOUR LIFE BE A LIGHT

In days gone by, the watchman would move through the city streets at nightfall crying, "Hang out your lights! Hang out your lights!"

In a real sense this is the task of every Christian and we have it laid out for us in Matthew 5:16: "Let your light shine before others, so that they may see your good works and give glory to your Father in heaven" (NRSV).

What does this mean? It means that our lives are to give light to the darkness around us as to glorify God. It means that in this sinful and wicked world, the children of God must shed light and thereby be a reflection of God's love and a window through which it might be seen by others.

In the days of Jesus, God had been obscured by the pagan cults and the demands of the state. Religion had grown to be more of a form than a force, and its legalistic interpretation had robbed it largely of spiritual meaning. So, God sent Jesus into the world to shed light and to dispel this darkness. Jesus came so that humankind might see God through him. His purpose was to draw humankind to God and to save them from their sins.

His disciples were to shine for his sake and aid in spreading light. They were to be reflectors of his light and thus multiply the light he came to bring. Now today, we who are followers of those early disciples are to shine for his sake so that God is glorified.

How are we to let our lights shine?

For one thing kindness can be a light that glorifies God, and unless there is kindness and love in all we do, our lights will be dim indeed. We cannot be a reflection of Christ unless we are kind.

Basic in all he did was this tenderness, compassion, and kindness. He rebuked people for their sins out of a heart of love. He sought to heal and not to hurt the wounded. It was this kindness and love which drew people to him and opened for them new understanding and appreciation of God.

To be reflectors of him, we too must be thoughtful and loving toward all around us. Meanness obscures God. Kindness reflects God.

Courage can be a light which glorifies God. Jesus faced dangerous situations and cruel people with calm courage. His dependence upon God let others know that they did not need to be afraid. His courage came from above.

See him there in the temple indignant over moneychangers who had made the house of God a marketplace. With righteous indignation he drove them out.

Today, when his followers stand for what is right against the odds of the crowd—by their courage a light glorifies God. When principle is followed in place of desire, when what is expedient gives way to what is right, then God's courage is reflected.

It is the courage of others which inspires and strengthens us to carry on. Courageous spirits are God's servants shining in a dark world.

Then, faith is a light which is contagious and which glorifies God. Jesus never wavered in trust in the Father. His was such a confidence in the love and mercy of God that people were lifted and drawn to him.

If we are to be lights which dispel the darkness of despair and mistrust, we must let our faith in the goodness and mercy of God be seen.

Ours must be a faith that is willing to do what the Lord requires of us—to follow the course of virtue, the path of justice; to defend the poor and the fatherless; to do justice to the afflicted and needy.

Wallace Fridy

WHAT DOES THE LORD REQUIRE OF YOU?

Table conversation often gives birth to interesting expressions and firm convictions. One evening we were visiting with a retired schoolteacher, a long-time family friend.

We were discussing the depressed economy in our native state when she remarked, "Everyone is entitled to a good pair of shoes and a mattress!" This reflected her years of teaching in an area where many students did not have "good" shoes and perhaps only a couch or cot to sleep on. Each day when she saw worn out shoes, it was a reminder that this is not the way things should be.

When persons of faith see such a situation, we hear anew the answer offered by the prophet regarding God's will: Have mercy and do justice. The response should involve some form of action both from the individual and from the collective efforts of the community. Such responses lead to walking in the way of the Lord.

Le Noir Culbertson

GOD, THE TRUE SHEPHERD

For thus says the Lord God: I myself will search for my sheep, and will seek them out. As shepherds seek out their flocks when they are among their scattered sheep, so I will seek out my sheep. I will rescue them from all the places to which they have been scattered on a day of clouds and thick darkness. I will bring them out from the peoples and gather them from the countries, and will bring them into their own land; and I will feed them on the mountains of Israel, by the watercourses, and in all the inhabited parts of the land. I will feed them with good pasture, and the mountain heights of Israel shall be their pasture; there they shall lie down in good grazing land, and they shall feed on rich pasture on the mountains of Israel. I myself will be the shepherd of my sheep, and I will make them lie down, says the Lord God. I will seek the lost, and I will bring back the strayed, and I will bind up the injured, and I will strengthen the weak, but the fat and the strong I will destroy. I will feed them with justice.

As for you, my flock, thus says the Lord God: I shall judge between sheep and sheep, between rams and goats: Is it not enough for you to feed on the good pasture, but you must tread down with your feet the rest of your pasture? When you drink of clear water, must you foul the rest with your feet? And must my sheep eat what you have trodden with your feet, and drink what you have fouled with your feet?

Therefore, thus says the Lord God to them: I myself will judge between the fat sheep and the lean sheep. Because you pushed with flank and shoulder, and butted at all the weak animals with your horns until you scattered them far and wide, I will save my flock, and they shall no longer be ravaged; and I will judge between sheep and sheep.

I will set up over them one shepherd, my servant David, and he shall feed them: he shall feed them and be their shepherd. And I, the Lord, will be their God, and my servant David shall be prince among them; I, the Lord, have spoken.

I will make with them a covenant of peace and banish wild animals from the land, so that they may live in the wild and sleep in the woods securely. I will make them and the region around my hill a blessing; and I will send down the showers in their season; they shall be showers of blessing. The trees of the field shall yield their fruit, and the earth shall yield its increase. They shall know that I am the Lord, when I break the bars of their yoke, and save them from the hands of those who enslaved them. They shall no more be plunder for the nations, nor shall the animals of the land devour them; they shall live in safety, and no one shall make them afraid. I will provide for them a splendid vegetation so that they shall no more be consumed with hunger in the land, and no longer suffer the insults of the nations. They shall know that I, the Lord their God, am with them, and that they, the house of Israel, are my people, says the Lord God. You are my sheep, the sheep of my pasture and I am your God, says the Lord God.

Ezekiel 34:11-31 NRSV

WHY CAN'T EVERYBODY JUST LIVE IN PEACE?

"Did too!"

"Did not!"

"Did too!"

"Did not!"

"Boys, that's enough," interrupted Mrs. Mitchell, the third grade teacher at Lewis and Clark School.

"He started it."

"No, I didn't. You did."

"Did not!"

"Did too!"

"I don't care who started it. I want it stopped right now! Is that clear?"

"Yes, Mrs. Mitchell," they replied in unison. If Mrs. Mitchell remembered correctly, this was the sixth shouting and shoving match at recess that week. And it was only Tuesday. A big sigh escaped from her mouth. When the students reassembled in the classroom, acting on a sudden inspiration, she gave them a written assignment. She printed on the chalkboard the following questions: "Why do kids fight so often? Why can't everybody just live in peace?"

After the usual moaning and groaning, the children settled down to work. That evening, in her slippers and robe, and with a cup of her favorite lemon tea, Mrs. Mitchell read their responses. She was pleasantly surprised by their candid and insightful answers.

"Kids fight for the same reasons adults fight—jealousy, hatred, and greed."

"Kids learn how to fight from watching adults. My parents are especially good teachers."

"Hitting people is easier than listening to them. Working things out is a lot harder than punching somebody out."

"When I'm quiet and nice, nobody pays any attention to me. But if I holler and scream, I get noticed real fast."

"I'd rather argue than admit I'm wrong."

"Sometimes, the reason people fight is they're scared. At least that's why I do."

"I like how it feels when I get even."

"I want my own way, and throwing a fit is the quickest way to get it. It works every time."

"My friends might think I'm a wimp if I didn't stand up for my rights."

Though their explanations are less complex, these are the same basic reasons nations fight. Attempting to justify their warlike actions, one group labels its reasons noble, while those of their adversaries are discredited and dismissed.

Admittedly, it's a perplexing and frustrating question. Why can't everybody just live together in peace? Why do humans fight so much and nations go to war so often?

Perhaps the human race is depraved and rotten to the core. Many would subscribe to this theory and would have us believe that, born in original sin and left to themselves, people can't quit their destructive, violent behavior.

There are also those who preach original blessing; who emphasize that we are born of love, possessing high hopes and filled with amazing potential. If this is so, fighting and wars are not inevitable. Instead, they're the product of the same destructive qualities those school children listed: fear that reveals itself in jealousy, bigotry, and prejudice; the unwillingness to forgive, the failure to be kind and gentle with one another; selfishness that rears its ugly head as greed and possessiveness; deep-seated hostility that produces racism and sexism.

Entire cultures store up and pass on to new generations ancient antagonisms whose original causes are but dimly perceived. Nevertheless, children often retain a refreshing idealism in spite of society's promotion of violence and injustice. Cynical adults (which may include most of us) know these youthful dreams are unrealistic and naive. Utopias have been tried again and again and have always failed. Growing up teaches us firsthand how tough and unyielding the big world can be.

But experience also reveals that the world's a wonderful place, overflowing with beauty and abundance; filled with caring, supportive persons; alive with creative possibilities. How we view reality becomes a matter of focus and perspective.

I choose to think that people could get along together; that wars are not decreed by fate or fixed in the eternal scheme of things. They're options we unwisely choose. Of course there'll always be minor disagreements. But every conflict could, in fact, be resolved, and the human race could live in peace, if everyone practiced radical servanthood as proclaimed and lived by Jesus of Nazareth.

Rather than train our children to be cynical and pessimistic, adults would be well-advised to learn idealism, optimism, wonder, and awe while sitting at their children's feet. A pinch of playfulness would help, too.

Kel Groseclose

THE GOOD SAMARITAN

But wanting to justify himself, he asked Jesus, "Jesus who is my neighbor?" Jesus replied, "A man was going down from Jerusalem to Jericho, and fell into the hands of robbers, who stripped him, beat him, and went away, leaving him half dead. Now by chance a priest was going down that road; and when he saw him, he passed by on the other side. So likewise a Levite, when he came to the place and saw him, passed by on the other side. But a Samaritan while traveling came near him; and when he saw him, he was moved with pity. He went to him and bandaged his wounds, having poured oil and wine on them. Then he put him on his own animal, brought him to an inn, and took care of him. The next day he took out two denarii, gave them to the innkeeper, and said, 'Take care of him; and when I come back, I will repay you whatever more you spend.' Which of these three, do you think, was a neighbor to the man who fell into the hands of the robbers?" He said, "The one who showed him mercy." Jesus said to him, "Go and do likewise."

Luke 10:29-37 NRSV

WHO SAYS SO?

A high-powered lawyer tried to put Jesus on the spot, hoping to make him look bad in front of his friends and students. "What do I have to do," he asked, "to get into heaven?" Jesus answered by asking two questions of his own.

"You've read what the scriptures say about it, haven't you? Well, what's your opinion?"

"I don't know. That's why I'm asking you. I'm familiar with those rules about loving God with all your heart and your neighbor as yourself. But I get confused. Who exactly is my neighbor?"

In order to make the answer clear and unforgettable, Jesus told the lawyer a story. It's called the parable of the good Samaritan. When he got to the punch line, which in its element of surprise surpassed anything O. Henry ever thought up, Jesus asked yet another question.

"Which of these three people, the priest, Levite, or Samaritan, proved to be a neighbor to the robbery victim?" The attorney responded with the obvious answer, the Samaritan. "Gotcha," said Jesus. "Now it's your turn to go into the world and act the same."

Jesus was skilled at gently but firmly dealing with folks who kept saying, "Who says so?" Like the lawyer, they used a variety of questions and were usually subtle about it. But their actual motives were transparent to Jesus. What they really wanted to ask was, "Where do you come off speaking for God?" And "Who do you think you are to criticize our religious practices and lifestyle?"

One of Jesus' frequent and favorite methods of answering a question was to ask a question. "Who says so?" was likely to get a "Why do you want to know?" in return. It placed responsibility where it belonged — with the person doing the asking. Jesus never avoided giving sincere answers to honest queries. Sometimes, though, he wanted to give inquirers the opportunity to answer their own questions. He knew they had the answers. They simply needed a perceptive person to draw out the truth already within them.

The authority of Jesus was inner and spiritual. He didn't recite long lists of rules and regulations, brag about going to a prestigious rabbinical school, or pull rank in any other way. He spoke from the heart. When somebody cornered him and asked, "Who says so?", Jesus never replied with a defensive, "I do, that's who!"

In daily family life, children frequently ask, "Who says so?" As annoying as this may be for busy, tired parents, it should be handled as graciously as possible. Avoid autocratic responses that cut off discussion, cause frustration, and build resentment. Save "Because I say so!" for dire emergencies only.

Borrow a page from the way of Jesus. Ask a question right back. It's a particularly effective and disarming approach, especially for potentially divisive topics. Before leaping to your own defense, find out what the other person feels, thinks, and believes.

"Who says so?" is basically a struggle to determine who's in charge. It's a fair question for people of all ages to ask. God has never seemed to be bothered by it, even when Old Testament prophets raised their clenched fists toward the heavens and demanded to know "How come?" As the ultimate authority in our lives, God is never authoritarian, arbitrary, or capricious. The Divine Being is wonderfully gentle and consistent.

Openness is a worthy goal for adults who live and work with children. A dogmatic approach may gain short-term results; but over the long haul, responses that engage other persons in decision making are far more productive. The desired objective is not the uncritical obedience of the small person to the big person. Rather it is helping individuals young and old alike attain their highest potential and achieve their maximum inner growth. The climate most conducive for this is one of mutual respect, honesty, freedom of expression, and trust.

We must all learn to accept external controls, checks, and balances. They're a reality at nearly every turn. However, if outward rules are our primary motivation, we will sooner or later become cranky, grouchy people. What we truly want for our children, our youth, and ourselves is the wisdom to turn all the "ought-to's" into "want-to's." Those who do are on their way to a life filled with deep relationships, rich experiences, and abiding joy.

Kel Groseclose

GETTING UPSET FOR THE RIGHT REASONS

If God and the angels do give a final exam in the life beyond this life, I know for a certainty what will not be on it. We shall not be asked, "Did you make your bed every morning before breakfast? Did you eat all your peas and carrots before you had dessert? How often did you clean beneath the stove? Did you change your socks and underwear every day?" I'm convinced the questions will rather concern the quality of our relationships, our willingness to give and serve, the depth of our compassion, the joy and comfort we brought to others. We shall not be asked, "Did the color and pattern of your shirt always match that of your pants? Was your hairdo ever more than three years out of style?"

We may well be asked, "Were you honest and fair in your business dealings? Did you treat poor and rich people equally? Did you love others for who they were on the inside and not according to any external characteristics such as skin tone, language, manner of dress, money in the bank, or place of residence?" If there is a heavenly entrance exam, it will surely include, "Were you true to your own best self, and to the best of your ability did you follow the leading of God's Spirit?"

Kel Groseclose

THE SAVIOUR

And there shall come forth a rod of the stem of Jesse, and a Branch shall grow out of his roots:

And the spirit of the Lord shall rest upon him, the spirit of wisdom and understanding, the spirit of counsel and might, the spirit of knowledge and of the fear of the Lord;

And shall make him of quick understanding in the fear of the Lord: and he shall not judge after the sight of his eyes, neither reprove after the hearing of his ears:

But with righteousness shall he judge the poor, and reprove with equity for the meek of the earth: and he shall smite the earth with the rod of his mouth, and with the breath of his lips shall he slay the wicked.

And righteousness shall be the girdle of his loins, and faithfulness the girdle of his reigns.

Isaiah 11:1-5 KJV

GOD IS BETTER THAN
HIS PLANS

They tell me that the most thoroughly read section of a daily newspaper is the Letters to the Editor. Several years ago I stumbled upon a letter that captured my interest. The writer (a person unknown to me) was registering her objection to a proposed law. To make her point she said, "A child conceived illegitimately is not in God's plan for procreation."

I understood what she was saying, and I agreed with her basic contention. I wish, as much as she did, that no children were conceived out of wedlock. In the purest, absolute sense, what the woman said is true. Such conceptions are not in God's plan. If everything in our world happened according to God's plan, I think each person would be born into a home where the parents were married and where the child would be loved—and where it would be reared with enough food to eat, proper medical care, and a chance for a good education. And also, with parents who would never make a mistake in rearing the child. But everything in our world isn't working the way God planned it.

But I'm happy to tell you that God is better than his plans. And while I wish everything in our world had gone according to God's plans, I must says that I am in awe of God, not so much for his wondrous plans as for the fact that he is better than those plans.

I'm thinking just now of a Jewish man named Elimelech and his wife, Naomi. They lived in bad times, in the period that is known in the Bible as the time of the judges, a period of particularly unstable government. To make it worse, nature conspired against them and famine swept the land. So Elimelech and Naomi did what would otherwise have been for them unthinkable; they moved to Moab.

It's always difficult for someone to migrate from one country to another. It means learning a whole new set of customs and feeling like an outsider—often an unwelcome outsider. But more was involved in this instance, a great deal more. For generations there had been enmity between the Israelites and the Moabites, an enmity which ran so deep that the Israelites were commanded, in the book of Deuteronomy, that they should not allow a Moabite to enter the assembly of their people; not even to the tenth generation (Deuteronomy 23:3). In truth, "tenth generation" was probably just a poetic way of saying *forever*. The Moabites were outsiders, and were meant to remain that way. Perhaps it was the only way the Israelites could maintain their ethnic purity. In any event, if you accept the thinking of the book of Deuteronomy, you have to conclude that this was God's plan.

Elimelech and Naomi were in such hard times that obedience to such a law was a luxury they couldn't afford, so with their two sons they moved to Moab. It must have been a terribly painful decision. Sometime thereafter, Elimelech died.

Even worse, the two young sons fell in love with Moabite girls and married them. Still more time passed by and the two young men died, leaving three widows, two of them quite young and the other in her middle or later years. It could hardly have been a more dismal picture, because in that time and place a woman without a husband, a father, or a brother couldn't hope to survive, unless perhaps it would be by prostitution.

You may well know the rest of the story. Naomi decided to return to her homeland, Israel, where she could hope to locate some distant relative who would be responsible for her. One daughter-in-law, Ruth, chose to go with her. It was a brave, loving, illogical decision, considering how unwelcome she would be. But in Israel she caught the eye and soon the affections of a well-to-do older man named Boaz. They married and had a child. That child became the grandfather of David, the greatest and most revered of Israel's kings.

Now it would surely seem that this wasn't according to the plans. A Moabite wasn't supposed to be accepted in Israel, not even to the tenth generation. Yet it turns out that this Moabite woman, Ruth, becomes the great-grandmother of the king Israel honored the most. And that's not all. When you get to the New Testament and read Matthew's list of Jesus' ancestry, you find that Ruth was an ancestress of the Messiah, Jesus our Lord.

All of which is to say that God is better than his plans.

Consider another Old Testament story. When this same David

was king of Israel, he became enamored with a beautiful woman who was, unfortunately, married. She was, in fact, the wife of one of David's premier army officers. David committed adultery with her; then, to cover his crime, he arranged for the death of her husband so he could marry her. Believe me, that isn't the way God plans things. And God's prophet, Nathan, told David as much in fierce and unmistakable terms. He said that the child who had been conceived in their illegitimate union would die, as it did.

This is an ugly story. It seems that no good, none whatsoever, could possibly come from it. But later David and Bathsheba had another son. This son was Solomon, who succeeded David as king of Israel and who is still referred to as the wisest man that ever lived.

I think that if you and I were running things, we might have written off the union of David and Bathsheba as a total loss. Their romance had been born in lust and illegitimacy and was nurtured in deceit and murder. None of this was the way God would plan it. But God redeemed the ugly situation, because God is always better than his plans.

The truth is, if God allowed himself to be fenced in by his plans, there wouldn't be much room for the development of our human story. As Madeleine L'Engle points out, the people of God aren't all good, moral people. Often they are people who do quite wicked things. Often the best thing that can be said for them, she continues, is that when they fail, they pick themselves up, with God's help, and try again.

But this means that there's a constant tension in the scriptures between quality and grace, or between expectation and performance. A tension, that is, between God's plan and what God does with what we human beings give him. The scriptures tell us to speak the truth, but Abraham and Sarah lied in order to save Abraham's life. Yet Abraham is described as "the friend of God." The Law said the people should love the Lord their God with all their heart, soul, mind, and strength (Deuteronomy 6:5), but the writer of 2 Chronicles says of King Amaziah that "he did what was pleasing to the Lord, but did it reluctantly (2 Chronicles 25:2 GNB). The seventh commandment says, "You shall not commit adultery," but the son of an adulterous relationship, Jephthah, became one of God's chosen instruments as a judge of Israel (Judges 11).

And that's the way the biblical record goes, chapter after chapter, Old Testament and New. God has a plan, and has commandments, and has divine expectations, but human beings fall short. Does God say, then, "These human beings have destroyed my dreams, so hereafter I'll use angels?" Not at all, thanks be to God! God seems rather to say, ten million times over, "Let's see what can be done with the confusion these human beings have given me." God's laws are strict, but God's character is gracious. God is better than his plans.

Does this give license for misconduct? Some people in the first century apparently thought so. They reasoned that if God's grace was demonstrated in mercy toward their sins, then the more they sinned, the more the grace of God would be seen (Romans 6:15ff). But I think most of us would offer a different testimony. We have found that the more surely we have experienced the grace of God, the more surely we want to live worthy of its glory and beauty.

Watch God, the artist, at work, and be astonished. I see an artist with a fresh canvas, a supply of oils. He produces a masterpiece, and I view it with awe. Now I see another canvas. A fumbling novice has been struggling with it, and despite his good and earnest intentions, he has made a mess of things. You might almost think his aim was confusion. As he looks in despair at what he has done, he wants to throw it all away; nothing can redeem such a sorry affair as this.

Instead, he asks the Master Artist to see if there's any hope at all for this chaotic combination of colors. Slowly, steadily, surely the Master works, until at last he produces a canvas of surprising beauty. I don't really think it is what he would have made of this canvas if he had been able to work it from the beginning, but I marvel that he has brought so much beauty out of what was once nothing but disaster and confusion.

I am more impressed by the skill of the Artist in the second instance than in the first. And of course that's what I mean when I say that God is better than his plans. He shows how wondrous a Master he is, not by what he does with a perfect page — something we seem never to give him! — but by the skill with which he takes our confusions and turns them into an astonishing measure of order and beauty.

The late William Barclay visited one day with a psychiatrist in a leading British mental hospital. Barclay expressed his envy of the psychiatrist, because he could so often see the results of his work. But the psychiatrist answered, "Let me tell you something. All that a psychiatrist can do is to strip a person naked until you get down to the essential person; and if the essential person is bad stuff, there is nothing he can do about it." Turning to Barclay as a cleric, he continued, "That's where you come in."

In recalling the conversation, Barclay said, "I think he meant, that is where *Jesus Christ* comes in" (William Barclay, *In the Hands of God*, 118).

And that's the point of all I'm saying. That's what Christian salvation is about, and that's something of what we mean by the grace of God.

There are times in life when a voice will tell you that you've ruined everything. Sometimes the voice will come from some human being, even a well-meaning one, and sometimes it will simply rise up within your own soul — and those are the times when the voice is most persuasive! The voice will sound logical, because from what you can see, you have for sure ruined things. And whatever the judgment the voice passes on you, it will seem fair enough, because when a person messes things up, he or she should expect to pay the penalty. The voice will also seem moral, like the words in the letter to the editor to which I referred earlier.

But however logical, just, and moral the voice may seem, I insist that it is the voice of the devil, because it is a voice which not only denies the grace of God, but which also seeks to keep us from recognizing that such grace exists. Even if such a statement is well-intended, it fails to reckon with the power of the Master Artist of the universe.

Because God is ready always, at our invitation, to take the canvas of our lives, corrupted both by our mistakes and also by the mistakes and sometimes the unkindness and cruelty of others, and to begin reworking the canvas.

What God gets in the end will not be what was originally planned, because the original plan, it seems to me, was for a Garden of Eden, a place of perfection. But it will be a wondrous sight, a redeemed life. And all through eternity you will want to sing a song of grace: God is better than his plans.

Ellsworth Kalas

MERCY, THE VIRTUE THAT SHINES

During the War Between the States, a young teenage boy enlisted to be a soldier for the Union army. But he was not ready. He was much too young, and when the time came for his first encounter with the enemy, he became terrified and ran away. He was caught, arrested, judged guilty of desertion and sentenced to be shot by a firing squad.

His parents wrote a letter to President Abraham Lincoln, pleading for mercy, pleading for a pardon for their young son. Touched by their letter, President Lincoln called for the facts and when he realized the situation, he overruled the death sentence and granted the teenager a full presidential pardon.

In his official statement explaining his action, Mr. Lincoln wrote these words: "Over the years . . . I have observed that it does not do a boy much good to shoot him!"

On another occasion some months later, as the Civil War was winding down and it was obvious that the Union would win, someone asked President Lincoln how he would treat the southerners after the war was over.

He answered, "Like they had never been away."

"But Mr. President," the questioner protested, "aren't we supposed to destroy our enemies?"

I love Abraham Lincoln's response: "Don't we destroy our enemies when we make them our friends?"

That is the quality of mercy, and that gracious, forgiving spirit is one of the things that so endeared Abraham Lincoln to America and made him one of the great leaders of history. He lived out the truth of the fifth Beatitude: "Blessed are the merciful, for they will receive mercy."

James W. Moore

THE GETTYSBURG ADDRESS

Four-score and seven years ago our fathers brought forth on this continent a new nation conceived in liberty, and dedicated to the proposition that all men are created equal. Now we are engaged in a great civil war, testing whether that nation or any nation so conceived and so dedicated can long endure. We are met on a great battlefield of that war. We have come to dedicate a portion of that field as a final resting place for those who here gave up their lives that that nation might live. It is altogether fitting and proper that we should do this. But, in a larger sense, we cannot dedicate, we cannot consecrate, we cannot hallow this ground. The brave men, living and dead, who struggled here, have consecrated it far above our poor power to add or detract. The world will little note nor long remember what we say here, but it can never forget what they did here. It is for us, the living, rather to be dedicated here to the unfinished work that they who fought here have thus far so nobly advanced. It is rather for us to be here dedicated to the great task remaining before us—that from these honored dead we take increased devotion to that cause for which they gave the last full measure of devotion; that we here highly resolve that these dead shall not have died in vain; that the nation, under God, shall have a new birth of freedom; and that the government of the people, by the people, for the people, shall not perish from the earth.

Abraham Lincoln

KING SOLOMON AND
THE ANTS

One morning the Queen of Sheba started back to her home in the South. King Solomon and all his court went with her to the gates of the city.

It was a glorious sight. The King and Queen rode upon white horses. The purple and scarlet coverings of their followers glittered with silver and gold.

The King looked down and saw an ant hill in the path before them.

"See yonder little people," he said; "do you hear what they are saying as they run about so wildly?

"They say, 'Here comes the King, men call wise, and good, and great. He will trample us under his cruel feet.' "

"They should be proud to die under the feet of such a King," said the Queen. "How dare they complain?"

"Not so, great Queen," replied the King.

He turned his horse aside and all his followers did the same.

When the great company had passed, there was the ant hill unharmed in the path.

The Queen said, "Happy, indeed, must be your people, wise King. I shall remember the lesson. He only is noble and great who cares for the helpless and weak."

Flora J. Cooke

HE LOOKED FOR JUSTICE

Scripture often records succinct observations tinged with sadness and irony. So it was with Isaiah and the other troubled prophets who heard God's call for justice, but found only the blood shed by those who were spiritually blind and morally corrupt.

Each spring for more than twenty years, millions of Earth's inhabitants have set aside a day known as Earth Day, a day to celebrate the Creation, a day to warn of neglect and misuse. Our century clearly has been one in which our stewardship of the earth's natural resources and healthy environment has been disappointing.

Where justice should have been done to the earth, we have seen its lifeblood shed through pollution, waste, and exploitation.

Clean air and water, abundant wildlife and vegetation, a harmonious existence with nature—these are our reminders in the first chapter of Genesis. "God saw all that he made, and it was very good" (v. 31). How often must we be reminded?

Barry Culbertson

TEMPERANCE

Temperance is a word that has fallen into disuse. We most often associate it with avoiding alcohol, but leading a temperate life means that we have achieved a balance between our creature comforts and our spiritual life. Simply put it means taking care not to go overboard or to do too much of anything. We shouldn't eat or drink too much or the wrong things; we shouldn't worry too much or about the wrong things; we should not talk too loudly or too long; and we shouldn't put too much importance on money and the things it can buy.

Since an overseer is entrusted with God's work, he must be blameless — not overbearing, not quick-tempered, not given to much wine, not violent, not pursuing dishonest gain. Rather he must be hospitable, one who loves what is good, who is self-controlled, upright, holy and disciplined. He must hold firmly to the trustworthy message as it has been taught, so that he can encourage others by sound doctrine and refute those who oppose it.

Titus 1:8-9 NIV

TEMPERANCE

Teach what is consistent with sound doctrine. Tell the older men to be temperate, serious, prudent, and sound in faith, in love, and in endurance.

Likewise tell the older women to be reverent in behavior, not to be slanderers or slaves to drink; they are to teach what is good, so that they may encourage the young women to love their husbands, to love their children, to be self-controlled, chaste, good managers of the household, kind, being submissive to their husbands, so that the word of God may not be discredited.

Likewise, urge the younger men to be self-controlled. Show yourself in all respects a model of good works, and in your teaching show integrity, gravity, and sound speech that cannot be censured; then any opponent will be put to shame, having nothing evil to say to us.

For the grace of God has appeared, bringing salvation to all, training us to renounce impiety and worldly passions, and in the present age to live lives that are self-controlled, upright, and godly, while we wait for the blessed hope and the manifestation of the glory of our great God and Savior, Jesus Christ. He it is who gave himself for us that he might redeem us from all iniquity and purify for himself a people of his own who are zealous for good deeds.

Titus 2:1-8, 11-14 NRSV

THE SILVER MINE

In a small village of Sweden there were once five men who went on a moose hunt. One of them was the parson; two were soldiers, named Eric and Olaf Swärd; the fourth man was the innkeeper and the fifth was a peasant named Israel Per Persson.

These men were good hunters who usually had luck with them; but that day they wandered long and far without getting anything. They grew much discouraged and had sat down to talk when the parson saw something that glittered where he had kicked away a moss-tuft. He picked up a sliver of stone that came with the moss and it shone exactly like the other. "It can't be possible that this stuff is lead," said he. Then the others sprang up and scraped away the turf with the butt end of their rifles. When they did this they saw plainly that a broad vein of ore followed the mountain. "What do you think this might be?" asked the parson. The men chipped off bits of stone and bit into them. "It must be lead, or zinc at least," said they. "And the whole mountain is full of it," added the innkeeper.

The clergyman and his companions were very happy; they fancied that now they had found that which would give them wealth. "I'll never have to do any more work," said one. "Now I can afford to do nothing at all the whole week through, and on Sundays I shall drive to church in a golden chariot!" They put back the moss-tuft to conceal the vein of ore. Then they carefully noted where the place was, and on the way home agreed that the parson should travel to Falun to ask the mining expert what kind of ore this was. He was to return as soon as possible, and until then they promised one another not to reveal to a single soul where the ore was to be found.

Then the parson departed with a few samples of ore in his pocket. He was just as happy in the thought of being rich as the others were. He would rebuild the parsonage and have a comfortable living. After driving two days he reached Falun and showed his bits of ore to the expert there.

"No, it's not lead," said the mineralogist.

"Perhaps it's zinc, then," said the parson.

"No, nor zinc, either."

The parson thought that all the hope within him sank. He had not been so depressed in many a long day.

"Have you many stones like this in your parish?" asked the mineralogist.

"We have a whole mountain full," said the parson.

Then the mineralogist came up closer, slapped the parson on the shoulder, and said, "Let us see that you make such good use of this that it will prove a blessing both to you and to the country, for it is silver."

❋ ❋ ❋ ❋ ❋ ❋ ❋

When the parson reached home again, he went first to tell his partners of the value of their find. Stopping at the innkeeper's gate, he noticed that evergreen was strewn all up the path to the door. "Who has died in this place?" he asked of a boy who was leaning against the fence.

"The innkeeper himself," answered the boy. "He had drunk himself full of brandy every day for a week. He said he had found a mine, and was very rich. He should never have to do anything now but drink, he said. Last night, he drove off, full as he was, and the wagon turned over and he was killed."

When the parson heard this, he drove homeward, much distressed, instead of being so happy over his good news, as he had been before. When he had driven a few paces, he saw Israel Per Persson walking along. Him he would cheer at once with the good news that he was a rich man. But when Per Persson heard that the ore was silver he began looking more and more mournful.

"Oh, is it silver?" he said again.

"Why, of course it is silver," replied the parson. "I would not deceive you. You must not be afraid of being happy."

"Happy!" said Per Persson. "Should I be happy? I believed it was only glitter that we had found, so I thought it would be better to take the certain for the uncertain. I have sold my share to Olaf Swärd for a hundred dollars." He was desperate, and when the parson left him, he stood on the highway and wept.

When the clergyman got back to his home, he sent a servant to tell Olaf and Eric that it was silver they had found. He thought he had had enough of spreading the good news himself. In the evening as he thought the whole matter over, he decided, "I will dream no more of bringing glory and profit to myself with these riches; but I can't let the silver lie buried in the earth! I must take it out, for the benefit of the poor and needy. I will work the mine, to put the whole parish on its feet."

So one day the parson went out to see Olaf Swärd, to ask him and his brother as to what should be done immediately with the silver mountain. When he came to the barracks, what was his amazement and grief to hear that Olaf and his brother had had such violent quarrels about the silver that Eric had been killed and Olaf was being sent away for long years of punishment.

"Promise me," said Olaf to the parson, "that you will watch over my children, and never let them have any portion of that which comes from the mine." The parson staggered back a step and was dumb. "If you do not promise, I cannot go in peace," said the prisoner.

"Yes," said the parson, slowly, "I will do as you ask."

On the way home he thought of the wealth which he had been so happy over. Was it really true that the people in this community could not stand riches? Already four were ruined, who hitherto had been dignified and excellent men. He pictured to himself how this silver mine would destroy one after another of the whole community. Was it fitting that he, who had been appointed to watch over these poor human beings' souls, should let loose upon them that which would be their destruction?

He called the peasants together to vote. He reminded them of all the misfortunes which the discovery of the mountain had brought upon them, and he asked them if they were going to let themselves be ruined or if they would save themselves. Then he told them that they must not expect him, their spiritual adviser, to help on their destruction. Now he had decided not to reveal to anyone where the silver mine was, and never would he himself take riches from it. If they wished to continue their search for the mine and wait upon riches, then he would go so far away that no hearsay of their misery could reach him. But if they would give up thinking about the silver mine, and be as before, he would remain with them. "Whichever way you may choose," said the parson, "remember this, that, from me, no one shall ever know anything about the silver mountain."

And the peasants decided that the parson should go to the forest and conceal the vein of ore with evergreen and stone, so that no one would be able to find it—neither themselves nor their posterity.

Long after, the land of Sweden was in great danger, and the parson thought it would be right to offer the King the secret of the mountain, that its wealth might be used for the defense of the realm. When the King heard all the story, "You must let the mine lie in peace," he said.

"But if the kingdom is in danger?" asked the parson.

"The kingdom is better served with men than with money," answered the King.

Condensed from The Girl from the Marsh Croft *by Selma Lagerlöf*

CONDUCT IN THE WORLD

Feb. 23, 1690

I am very glad, Madame, to hear that at last you have contrived to secure some solitary hours. Postponing the hour for seeing people as late as may be, and sometimes seeking shelter elsewhere — these are both good ways of defending yourself from importunate visitors. And at other times you may well cut short your intercourse with people whose only aim is amusement or unnecessary business. As to daily matters which appertain to your duties, or to providential arrangements, you can but put up with them patiently, however inconvenient or disturbing. It is a great consolation to remember that God is often hidden behind such disturbing conditions, as well as behind the most edifying friendships. Behind each importunate intruder learn to see God governing all, and training you in self-denial alike through a troublesome acquaintance as through the edifying examples of real friends. The former thwarts our will, upsets our plans, makes us crave more earnestly for silence and recollection, teaches us to sit loose to our own arrangements, our ease, our taste, our rest: he trains us to bend our will to that of others, to humble ourselves when impatience gets the better of us under such annoyance, and kindles a greater longing after God, even while He seems to be forsaking us because we are so disturbed.

I do not mean that we ought voluntarily to put ourselves in the way of dissipating influences: God forbid! That would be tempting God and seeking danger; but such disturbances as come in any way providentially, if met with due precaution and carefully guarded hours of prayer and reading, will turn to good. Whatever comes from God's Hand bears good fruit. Often those things which make you sigh after solitude are more profitable to your humiliation and self-denial that the most utter solitude itself would be. Let us be content to live day by day as God leads us, making good use of every moment, without looking beyond it. Sometimes an exciting book, a fervent meditation, or a striking conversation, may flatter your tastes and make you feel self-satisfied and complacent, fancying yourself far advanced towards perfection, and, by filling you with unreal notions, be all the while only swelling your pride, and making you come forth from your religious exercises less tolerant towards whatever crosses your will. I would have you hold fast to this simple rule: seek nothing dissipating, but bear quietly with whatever God sends without your seeking it, whether of dissipation or interruption. It is a great delusion to seek God afar off, in matters perhaps altogether unattainable, ignoring that He is beside us amid our daily annoyances so long as we bear humbly and bravely all those which arise from the manifold imperfections of our neighbours and ourselves.

I have but one word to say to you concerning love for your neighbour, namely, that nothing save humility can mould you to it; nothing but the consciousness of your own weakness can make you indulgent and pitiful to that of others. You will answer, "I quite understand that humility should produce forbearance towards others, but how am I first to acquire humility?" Two things combined will bring that about; you must never separate them. The first is contemplation of the deep gulf whence God's All-powerful Hand has drawn you out, and over which He ever holds you, so to say, suspended. The second is the Presence of that All-penetrating God. It is only in beholding and loving God that we can learn forgetfulness of self, measure duly the nothingness of that which has dazzled us, and accustom ourselves thankfully to "decrease" (John 3:30) beneath that Great Majesty which absorbs all things. Love God, and you will be humble; love God, and you will throw off the love of self; love God, and you will love all that He gives you to love for love of Him.

François de Salignac de la Moth Fénelon

THE PROUD OAK TREE

The oak said to the reed that grew by the river: "It is no wonder that you make such a sorrowful moaning, for you are so weak that the little wren is a burden for you, and the lightest breeze must seem like a storm-wind. Now look at me! No storm has ever been able to bow my head. You will be much safer if you grow close to my side so that I may shelter you from the wind that is now playing with my leaves."

"Do not worry about me," said the reed; "I have less reason to fear the wind than you have. I bow myself, but I never break. He who laughs last, laughs best!"

That night there came a fearful hurricane. The oak stood erect. The reed bowed itself before the blast. The wind grew more furious, and, uprooting the proud oak, flung it on the ground.

When the morning came there stood the slender reed, glittering with dewdrops, and softly swaying in the breeze.

From Deutsches Drittes Lesebuch,
by W. H. Weick and C. Grebner.

DEGREES OF HUMILITY

The first degree of humility is to submit and humble myself, so far as I can, so that in all things I obey the law of God. My obedience should be such that, even if I were made emperor of the entire world, I would still simply try to obey the divine laws, for the sake of my own salvation.

The second degree of humility is more perfect than the first. It consists in attaining such a state that I neither desire, nor am affected by, riches rather than poverty, honour rather than dishonour, a long life rather than a short life. This can only be attained when the services of God and the salvation of my soul have equal importance to me. By this means I shall never want to commit any sin, both for offending God, and also for my own sake.

The third degree is the most perfect humility. This is when, in order to imitate Christ more fully, and actually become like him, I desire and choose the poverty of Christ, rather than riches; I choose to be treated with the same contempt with which Christ was treated, rather than pursue honour; I choose to be regarded as useless and foolish for Christ's sake, who was himself dismissed as useless and foolish, rather than be judged wise and prudent by this world.

Ignatius of Loyola
from *The Spiritual Exercises*
1491–1556

PERSONAL TEMPERANCE

Do you not know that your body is a temple of the Holy Spirit, who is in you, whom you have received from God? You are not your own; you were bought at a price. Therefore honor God with your body.

Therefore, I urge you, brothers, in view of God's mercy, to offer your bodies as living sacrifices, holy and pleasing to God—which is your spiritual worship. Do not conform any longer to the pattern of this world, but be transformed by the renewing of your mind. Then you will be able to test and approve what God's will is—his good, pleasing and perfect will.

Be careful, then, how you live—not as unwise but as wise, making the most of every opportunity, because the days are evil. Therefore do not be foolish, but understand what the Lord's will is. Do not get drunk on wine, which leads to debauchery. Instead, be filled with the Spirit.

Who has woe? Who has sorrow?
    Who has strife? Who has complaints?
    Who has needless bruises? Who has bloodshot eyes?
Those who linger over wine,
    who go to sample bowls of mixed wine.
Do not gaze at wine when it is red,
    when it sparkles in the cup,
    when it goes down smoothly!
In the end it bites like a viper
    and poisons like a viper.
Do not join those who drink too much wine
    or gorge themselves on meat,
for drunkards and gluttons become poor,
    and drowsiness clothes them in rags.

So, if you think you are standing firm, be careful that you don't fall! If anyone destroys God's temple, God will destroy him; for God's temple is sacred, and you are that temple.

So I say, live by the Spirit, and you will not gratify the desires of the sinful nature.

1 Corinthians 6:19-20; Romans 12:1-2;
Ephesians 5:15-18; Proverbs 23:29-32, 20-21;
1 Corinthians 10:12; 3:17; Galatians 5:16 NIV

Runaway

I am like a beggar in the streets, like a runaway child
    caught in a web of abuse.
Surely, O God, you will not pass me by; you will not
    count me worthless.
Your ear, O Holy One, hears the cry of the least of
    your creatures; you have chosen the humble and
    downcast for your very own.
With wild audacity I call upon you, the Ruler of Time
    and Space: Do not withhold your presence from
    one who is troubled beyond endurance.

All the world knows my fault; guilt has scarred both
    body and spirit.
You have seen the plight of your servant, O Unseen
    Power, and you know the condition of my heart.
I come before you, O Sovereign God, without
    reservation; ravaged and hurt, I have no defense
    except your covenant-promise.
Because you have forgiven, I dare to confess; because
    you have canceled my iniquity, I have the courage
    to hope.
My hope springs from the Ground of Being, my
    confidence from the history of a forgiven people.
The testimony is this: Yahweh our God is eternally
    bound, bound to creation in spite of sin; in spite
    of loneliness and atrocity, injustice and pain.
Yahweh our God chose the universe into being, and
    the Lord decreed an everlasting bond with all that
    was made.
My hope arises from covenant-promise, my confidence
    from the One who protects the world like a
    defiant mother bear.

O my people, do not turn away from God. Do not
   trust in human strength, or in your own
   competitive edge.
Stand vulnerable before the Mystery, the Lord of Life.
   Surely we will see the splendor of new possibility
   appear like sudden lightning.
Shout from radio towers and churches and cornfields:
   God is with us. As blessing and judgment and
   living presence, Yahweh is with us.
God hears the wretched cries of every forsaken
   creature. And God has brought each one safely
   across the Red Sea.
And each one will be carried safely across the barrier of
   death, and each one is safeheld in the profound
   forever-embrace of Yahweh our God.

Martin Bell

THE LITTLE PINE TREE WHO WISHED FOR NEW LEAVES

A little pine tree grew in the forest. It was not happy because it did not have leaves like the maple, oaks, and other trees that grew near.

"Why must I have only green needles on my branches?" it sighed. "How I wish that I might have leaves of shining gold and be different from all the other trees in the forest."

Now, the angel of the forest heard the little pine tree, and that night while it slept, its wish came true. The next morning the little pine tree had leaves of shining gold, and was very happy.

"How beautiful I am!" it thought. "What must the other trees think of me now!"

How foolish was the little pine tree! In the night a man came to the woods. He picked every one of the gold leaves and put them in a box.

"What shall I do?" cried the little tree. "I see now that it will not do to have leaves of gold. If I could only have leaves of glass, I would be happy again."

The angel of the forest, who was listening, again granted the little tree's wish, and the next morning when it awoke its branches were covered with leaves of clear, shining glass. Again the little tree was happy, but not for long. After a while the sunbeams hid and clouds gathered in the sky. Lower and lower they hung, and by and by the rain came. How the wind did blow! The glass leaves shook in the wind, and struck against the branches and against one another. Soon the leaves were shattered, and little bits of glass covered the ground. Not a leaf was left on the branches!

"Ah, me!" sighed the little tree again. "Perhaps I should not wish to be better than the other trees. If I could only have green leaves like theirs, I would be happy."

A third time the angel of the forest granted the little tree's wish. When morning came it was covered with big shiny green leaves. By and by a goat came along and ate every one of the nice juicy leaves for his dinner.

"Dear me!" said the little tree. "Perhaps it is best after all that I have only my green needles! If I could only have them back!"

While it slept that night the angel of the forest touched it and the next morning it awoke to find long green needles covering its branches. "I like the needles better than the gold, or the glass, or the green leaves," said the pine tree. The little pine never complained again. The birds were happy, too, for in the winter it was the little pine tree that kept them safe and warm.

THE THREE HEAVY STONES

On a lonely desert, amid barren and almost inaccessible rocks, Ben Achmet led a life of austerity and devotion. A cave in the rock was his dwelling. Roots and fruits, the scanty products of the sterile region he inhabited, satisfied his hunger, and a small spring that bubbled up from the lower part of a neighboring cliff slaked his thirst.

As years went by the fame of his sanctity spread abroad. He often supplied the traveler of the desert from his little spring. In times of pestilence, he left his solitary abode to attend to the sick and comfort the dying in the villages that were scattered around. His name inspired veneration and plundering armies gave up their booty at his command.

Akaba was a robber; he had a band of lawless men under his command, ready to do his bidding. He had a treasure-house stored with ill-gotten wealth, and a large number of prisoners. The sanctity of Ben Achmet arrested his attention; his conscience smote him on account of his guilt, and he longed to be famed for his devotion as he had been for his crimes.

He sought out Ben Achmet and told him of his desires. "Ben Achmet," said he, "I have five hundred men ready to obey me, numbers of slaves at my command, and a treasure-house filled with riches; tell me how to add to all of these the hope of a happy immortality."

Ben Achmet led him to a neighboring cliff that was steep, rugged, and high, and pointing to three large stones that lay near together, told him to lift them from the ground, and to follow him up the cliff. Akaba, laden with the stones, could scarcely move; to ascend the cliff with the stones was impossible. "I can not follow you, Ben Achmet," he said, "with these burdens." "Then cast down one of the stones," replied Ben Achmet, "and hasten after me." Akaba dropped one of the stones, but still found himself too heavily encumbered to proceed.

"I tell you it is impossible," cried the robber chieftain; "you yourself could not climb with such a load." "Let go of another stone, then," said Ben Achmet.

Akaba readily dropped another stone, and with great difficulty, clambered the cliff for awhile, till, exhausted with the effort, he again cried out that he could come no further. Ben Achmet directed him to drop the last stone, and no sooner had he done this, than he ran the rest of the way to the summit where Ben Achmet waited.

"My Son," said Ben Achmet, "You have three burdens which stand in your way to a better world. Disband your troops of lawless plunderers, set your prisoners at liberty, and restore your ill-gotten wealth to its owners; it is easier for you to climb to the top of this cliff with three large stones than it would be for you to journey onward to a better world with the power, pleasure, and riches in your possession."

Anonymous
New School Reader

HUMILITY AND EXALTATION

Who hath believed our report? and to whom is the arm of the Lord revealed?

For he shall grow up before him as a tender plant, and as a root out of a dry ground: he hath no form nor comeliness; and when we shall see him, there is no beauty that we should desire him.

He is despised and rejected of men; a man of sorrows, and acquainted with grief: and we hid as it were our faces from him; he was despised, and we esteemed him not.

Surely he hath borne our griefs, and carried our sorrows: yet we did esteem him stricken, smitten of God, and afflicted.

But he was wounded for our transgressions, he was bruised for our iniquities; the chastisement of our peace was upon him; and with his stripes we are healed.

All we like sheep have gone astray; we have turned every one to his own way; and the Lord hath laid on him the iniquity of us all.

He was oppressed, and he was afflicted, yet he opened not his mouth: he is brought as a lamb to the slaughter, and as a sheep · before her shearers is dumb, so he openeth not his mouth.

He was taken from prison and from judgment: and who shall declare his generation? for he was cut off out of the land of the living: for the transgression of my people was he stricken.

And he made his grave with the wicked, and with the rich in his death; because he had done no violence, neither was any deceit in his mouth.

Let the mind be in you, which was also in Christ Jesus:

Who, being in the form of God, thought it not robbery to be equal with God:

But made himself of no reputation, and took upon him the form of a servant, and was made in the likeness of men:

And being found in fashion as a man, he humbled himself, and became obedient unto death, even the death of the cross.

Wherefore God also hath highly exalted him, and given him a name which is above every name:

That at the name of Jesus every knee should bow, of things in heaven, and things in earth, and things under the earth;

And that every tongue should confess that Jesus Christ is Lord, to the glory of God the Father.

Isaiah 53:1-9; Philippians 2:5-11 KJV

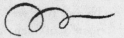

ROYAL LESSONS

It all began with a question, one that I asked my ten-year-old son, Richard.

"Are you gonna sign up for baseball this year?"

He fielded my loaded question quite deftly.

"It's too late. The sign-up date has already passed. They circulated the forms a week ago."

I was disappointed. I let it show with my next question.

"Want me to see if anything can be done?"

His enthusiastic answer surprised me.

"Hey, you think you could do that?"

"I can give it a try."

He smiled. "That's great!"

Had he picked up on my disappointment? Probably. Was he doing it just for me? I don't want to think so.

I called the Commissioner the next day. No dice. All of the teams were filled. There was nothing he could do.

"I'll call you if anything opens," he assured me.

I broke the news to Richard. He seemed distressed, but we soon moved on to something else. Another week passed, maybe more. I had forgotten all about baseball when a call came from the Commissioner.

"We have an opening," he said.

"We'll take it!"

"The Royals are having a practice game at 4:30 Thursday," he went on. "Your boy will be on that team."

"We'll be there!"

When I told Richard, he seemed to be as happy as I was. Neither of us wondered why there was an opening, or worried about the fact that Richard had missed the entire pre-season practice time. We had a spot on a team!

We arrived at the field right on time. Richard climbed out of the car and went to check in with his new coach and his new teammates. I climbed out, too, then stood there totally bewildered and stared at the field where the Royals were warming up.

I don't know which was the biggest shock, the coaches or the team itself. Neither one fit the image I had built up in my mind. Not in the least.

There's no way to deny it. I had hoped the Royals would be a championship-caliber team, appropriately dressed, well drilled, and finely polished, thanks to the two weeks of practice we had missed. And I had envisioned the coaches as dignified baseball veterans, barking out orders through stern, jutting jaws, surveying their charges through piercing eyes.

I wasn't prepared for the Royals.

I'll begin with the coaches.

How can I describe them? They were musicians by trade, which is nothing unusual in Nashville, but they actually *looked* like musicians, and somehow that didn't play well on the baseball diamond. Coach Johnny had long hair and a moustache. Coach Mike sported a bushy perm. And the considerable paunch that both of them carried didn't suggest that either had played any serious baseball lately. They weren't wearing the team's uniforms, either, and Coach Mike wore his cap backwards so it looked like a skullcap. A mass of curly hair stuck out around the edges. The net effect was something akin to a blue-hatted Bozo the Clown.

It wasn't just appearances, though. The coaches' exchanges were something out of a situation comedy. When we arrived they were arguing over which of them would pick up the team's new jerseys the next day. To hear them talk about it, you would find it hard to believe that either of them had any enthusiasm for the task ahead. It was downright slapstick, reminiscent of a routine by Abbott and Costello.

But the coaches were only half the problem. The other half was the team itself. The Bad News Bears looked like professionals by comparison.

"No wonder there's a spot available," I mumbled to myself. "I'm surprised they haven't *all* quit."

I turned my attention to the opponent of the day. As luck would have it, their slim, svelte coaches were decked out in immaculate uniforms that matched their team's spiffy, regulation attire, and their players were disciplined, organized, and ready to play. That team was lean and mean. The Royals were chunky and funky.

Richard stood on the outer edge of the group. He glanced my

way and shrugged his shoulders. But he had a sheepish smile on his face and didn't seem nearly as upset as I was.

Unfortunately, the game itself did little to boost my morale. Nothing went right. Fly balls dropped harmlessly in front of, or sometimes behind, our hapless outfielders. A routine grounder went for extra bases as the ball skittered through the legs of our shortstop. Several runs scored when one of our infielders threw the ball way over the first baseman's head. Our players actually *collided* with each other several times. Wild throws were the order of the day. When our team finally came up to bat, the few hits we made ended up as outs as we foolishly attempted to stretch beyond our abilities, running the bases with misguided abandon.

It was hopeless. Worse than that, it was a total embarrassment. I wanted to crawl off somewhere and hide while the score mounted for the other team.

I didn't hide, though. I stood there on the sidelines and toughed it out. And at some point during the afternoon I figured out what was *really* going on.

When did the truth dawn on me? I don't know for sure. Was it during the game, when our guys laughed together, encouraged one another, and horsed around the way guys do when they're having fun? They actually *enjoyed* one another.

Was it after the game, when the coaches gathered the boys around them and told them about the *good* things they had seen on that field? They challenged them to do better, yet they talked to them in such a way as to encourage them in spite of the loss. In the process, they managed to make those boys feel good about themselves.

Maybe it happened on the way home, when I heard the laughter in Richard's voice as he recounted the hilarious things that had happened during the game.

Maybe it was at dinner that night, when I saw the excitement in his eyes as he told his sisters how much *real fun* he'd had that afternoon, or when I overheard him telling his mother how welcome those guys had made him feel, that rag-tag bunch of rascals and their comic duo of coaches.

I can't say when it happened, but some time during that day I realized that my priorities were all mixed up and my impressions were all wrong. The day had been a total success for Richard. It had been filled with pleasure, not pain. It had been fun, not tense and pressured. He was actually looking forward to the remainder of the season!

Therein lies the first lesson I learned from the Royals. Never make a judgment on the basis of a first impression. Don't make decisions based on superficial knowledge and inadequate facts. To put it bluntly, you could be wrong.

I *was* wrong about the Royals in every possible respect. The coaches weren't misfits; they were unpolished jewels, and they taught my son lessons I *still* haven't fully learned. The players weren't rag-tag and disorganized; they were *boys*! Boys having fun, having a ball, as a matter of fact. And if I had actually acted on my first impression, Richard might have missed the wonderful experience of a season filled with fun.

Richard also would have missed a season filled with the thrill of victory, since that disorganized group of crazies ended up pulling together and turning into a team!

They began to come together after the fourth or fifth game. That's when they finally notched their first victory, which showed them what they were capable of doing. Their one-game winning streak stretched into two, then three, then four. Winning was contagious, and this little team, the one the other teams had written off as dead, began to make a difference in the league.

They climbed out of the cellar and began to claw their way upward toward respectability. As the season wore on, there was even talk about making it to the playoffs! One by one, they met and defeated the teams that had clobbered them during the first half of the season. Game by game, the other teams came to realize that the Royals were for real.

Fortunately, victory didn't spoil things. Our guys' attitudes never changed. The Bad News Bears were alive and well, still laughing at their own mistakes, still giving each other high fives, still having fun. Winning added a new dimension, to be sure, but the team still looked as if it belonged on a sandlot instead of a diamond. Coach Johnny's hair still flapped in the breeze, and Coach

Mike kept on wearing his cap backwards, on top of his perm. More important, the coaches and players kept on encouraging, praising, and supporting each other, win or lose.

During this crucial stretch, the Royals played a game against the league-leaders — I'll call them the Astros, although I no longer recall which team it actually was. I do remember they were the picture of perfection: sparkling clean uniforms with everything in place, regulation equipment, good-looking players who were well drilled and ready to play — they were marching toward an inevitable championship, grim-faced and dedicated, without the trace of a smile. And their coaches were baseball-wise and determined to win.

The league-leading team had a star. He was a big kid, nearly six feet tall, strikingly handsome, well coordinated, with a smooth, powerful swing and an innate ability to play almost any position with skill. He was the kind of boy every team but ours seemed to have, only he was the best of the best.

I knew the lad, and I knew his parents. His father was one of their coaches. Every time the boy came up to bat, the father-coach had a great deal to say. Nothing offensive, really, just a constant stream of instructions and criticisms, untempered by words of praise. The instructions were meant to be helpful, and so were the criticisms, but the overall effect was one of intense pressure.

The boy's mother was no better. We sat together, and before the game she spent a great deal of time telling Barbara and me stories about her son's success and predicting what he was likely to do against our team. And every time he came up to bat and failed to live up to her expectations, she apologized as if she'd personally done something wrong.

The net effect was sickening. It was a classic case of parents going overboard.

The game was a classic. The lead swapped back and forth in the early innings, and by the time the Astros woke up to reality, the Royals had the momentum.

In the bottom of the ninth, the Royals had the lead by two runs. The Astros were up. There were two outs, and two men were on base. As luck would have it, super son came up to bat. Super dad was incredibly tense. The game hung in the balance; his reputation was on the line.

Super dad paced the dugout like a panther, glaring at the boy, shouting out commands as if the lad could perform on demand. Super mom grimaced. She gripped the arms of her folding chair until her knuckles turned white. I could almost hear her teeth grinding together.

The boy popped the first pitch straight up. It was an obvious out. The game was as good as over. He trotted dejectedly toward first base in a half-hearted lope. As soon as the ball was caught, he left the base path and turned toward the dugout.

The Royals went crazy!

I didn't see that family for a few minutes. I was busy congratulating our guys on a huge, unexpected victory. But a while later, as the field was clearing and the players and their families were beginning to drift off, I saw all three of them. They were standing toe to toe. Mom and Dad were facing the boy. He was backed up against one of the light poles and was hemmed in. He had no place to go. He was trapped.

Mom and Dad were red-faced and agitated. They were looking up into the young lad's face, chewing him out. I couldn't hear their words, but I could tell what was happening. As for the boy, he just stood there, tall and proud, expressing no feeling, giving no response.

I had to walk past where they were standing in order to get to my car. As I approached, the two parents stopped talking. For the first time, the boy had an opportunity to respond. And when he did, it was all I could do to keep from kicking my heels together and shouting out loud.

Without changing his expression, without the slightest hint of sarcasm or disrespect, but with an uncanny measure of wisdom and insight, he looked down at his frustrated parents and summed it all up.

"It's just a game," he said quietly.

With those words, the boy delivered the second royal lesson.

For everything there is a season, the Bible tells us. There's a time for every matter under the sun. A time to be born, a time to die, a time for everything in between, including, I submit, a time to have fun. Sure, victory is important. So is effort, improvement, giving your best, and all the rest of it. But in the final analysis, when the *games* of life stop being fun, when they become a consuming passion, something is wrong.

Well, the season drew to a close. The Royals went to the playoffs and made it to the championship game. In that contest, it all came down to the bottom of the final inning. The other team, I'll call them the Cardinals, was ahead by one, but the Royals were at bat. There were two outs, the bases were loaded, and young Richard was coming up to bat. If they could get him out, the Cardinals would be champions!

The Cardinals put in a new pitcher. After he had finished warming up, Richard stepped into the batter's box.

"Time out!"

It was Coach Mike, calling out from his spot along the third-base line. He motioned for Richard to come his way. Strategy was all-important now.

Richard and Coach Mike met halfway between third base and home plate. Coach Mike put his arm around Richard's shoulder as they conferred. Richard looked serious as he listened to the man he had come to respect and admire so much. When the conference ended, Richard returned to the batter's box.

The pitcher leaned forward and glared toward the catcher.

"Time out!"

It was Coach Mike again. He motioned Richard over for another conference. Again they stood facing each other. Again Coach Mike's perm bounced up and down as he animatedly whispered instructions to his young charge.

I was dying inside. What was he telling him? The tension was killing me!

Richard returned to the batter's box. The pitcher wound up, paused, eyed the runners, and let it fly. Richard brought the bat around just as the right instant. With a resounding crack, the ball sailed down the third-base line! The third baseman lunged and missed. Two runs quickly scored. Richard raced to first and vaulted onto the bag, where he was mobbed by his overjoyed teammates!

Later, when the celebration had subsided and the Royals had carried off the coveted championship trophy, I asked Richard what Coach Mike had said to him during those two conferences.

"He told me not to swing at the first pitch."

"He said that both times?"

"Yep. Don't swing at the first pitch, no matter what. Let him throw one and see what he's got."

"But . . . you . . ."

Richard knew what I was thinking. He grinned sheepishly.

"Dad, I was *never* gonna get a better pitch than that!"

I smiled, too.

"What did coach say after the game?"

"He said, 'Attaboy, Rich.' "

"That's all?"

"That's all."

Good man, I thought. *Very* good man.

Royal lesson number three. God was smart enough to give childhood to children. We adults need to be smart enough to let them *keep* it, and smart enough to encourage them to enjoy it. After all, they're the ones who know what to do with it. And there'll be plenty of time to attend to the details later.

Richard Speight

GLORY IN CONTEMPT

One day in the winter, as St. Francis was coming to St. Mary of the Angels from Perugia with Brother Leo, who was walking a bit ahead of him, he said: "Brother Leo, even if the Friars Minor in every country should give a great example of holiness and integrity and good edification, nevertheless write down and note carefully that perfect joy is not in that."

And going on a bit, St. Francis cried out again in a strong voice: "Brother Leo, if a Friar Minor knew all languages and all sciences and Scripture, if he also knew how to prophesy and to reveal not only the future but also the secrets of the consciences and minds of others, write down and note carefully that perfect joy is not in that."

Now when he had been talking this way for a distance of two miles, Brother Leo in great amazement asked him: "Father, I beg you in God's name to tell where perfect joy is."

And St. Francis replied: "When we come to St. Mary of the Angels, soaked by the rain and frozen by the cold, all soiled with mud and suffering from hunger, and we ring at the gate of the Place and the brother porter comes and says angrily: 'Who are you?' And we say: 'We are two of your brothers.' And he contradicts us saying: 'You are not telling the truth. Rather, you are two rascals who go around deceiving people and stealing what they give to the poor. Go away!' And he does not open the door for us, but makes us stand outside in the snow and rain, cold and hungry, until night falls—then if we endure all those insults and cruel rebuffs patiently, without being troubled and without complaining, and if we reflect humbly and charitably that that porter really knows us and God makes him speak against us, oh, Brother Leo, write that perfect joy is there! . . .

"And if later, suffering intensely from hunger and the painful cold, with night falling, we still knock and call, and crying loudly beg them to open for us and let us come in for the love of God, and he grows still more angry and says: 'Those fellows are bold and shameless ruffians. I'll give them what they deserve!' And he comes out with a knotty club, and grasping us by the cowl throws us to the ground, rolling us in the mud and snow, and beats us with that club so much that he covers our bodies with wounds — if we endure all those evils and insults and blows with joy and patience, reflecting that we must accept and bear the sufferings of the Blessed Christ patiently for love of Him, oh, Brother Leo, write: that is perfect joy!

"And now hear the conclusion, Brother Leo. Above all the graces and the gifts of the Holy Spirit which Christ grants to His friends is that of conquering oneself and willingly enduring sufferings, insults, humiliations, and hardships for the love of Christ. For we cannot glory in all those other marvelous gifts of God, as they are not ours but God's, as the Apostle says: 'What have you that you have not received?'"

But we can glory in the cross of tribulations and afflictions, because that is ours, and so the Apostle says: "I will not glory save in the Cross of our Lord Jesus Christ."

Francis of Assisi
1181–1226

CUSTODIANSHIP

A friend of mine is a highly skilled engineer, and his company once sent him and his wife to live temporarily in Paris, whence he was able to travel easily to jobs all over Europe. When the couple left their home on Long Island, they were pleased to place it in the care of a middle-aged woman who had excellent references and promised to look after it as if it were her own.

Indeed, she did look after it as if it were her own. When she grew tired of the color of the kitchen, she repainted it to suit herself. When she decided she didn't like the wallpaper, she took a can of paint and redesigned it to her own taste. When the thought struck her that the exposed beams on the ceiling did not appear old enough, she took a hatchet and proceeded to "age" them. And when my friends' tour of duty was ended and they returned to the States to reclaim their home, she had become so convinced it was hers that she refused to leave. A court order and a sheriff were necessary to remove her!

"The nerve!" we say. "How would anyone have the gall to behave that way about property that was not hers?"

Yet this is precisely the point of Jesus' story about the vineyard. The owner of the vineyard left it in the care of tenants who forgot who it belonged to. Three times the owner sent servants to collect his profits from the vineyard, and each time the tenants beat the servants and sent them away. Finally the owner sent his son to collect, thinking surely they would not treat his son that way. But when the tenants saw the son, they thought, "The old man must be dead, and now his son is trying to collect. If we dispose of him, the vineyard will be ours and nobody will know the difference." So they killed the son (Luke 20:9-15).

Careless Custodians: A Recurring Theme

We would like to think that Jesus was talking about Israel and its rejection of the Messiah. Perhaps, at one level, he was. But the context in the Gospel of Luke suggests that there are other levels of the story as well. In fact, there is hardly a chapter of the Gospel, from the midpoint on, that does not contain a reference to the way we all tend to forget who the earth belongs to and how we ought to live on it.

First, in chapter 12, there is Jesus' story of the rich man whose crops grew in such abundance that he was preparing to build great storage barns to hold them, and then live the rest of his life in ease and luxury. But suddenly his heart gave out and he died. Then God said, "Now whose will these things be?" (16-21).

In chapter 15 is the story of the young man who asked for his inheritance early, took it abroad, and lost everything. Fortunately, the story has a happy ending, up to a point, for the young man finally sees the light and returns to his father's house (12-24).

In chapter 16 there are two stories—one is about a wicked custodian who realizes his master is about to cast him out of the house, and so he scurries about, making amends as fast as he can; the other is about a rich man who dies and wakes up in hell because he neglected the poor sick man who lay at his gate begging alms (1-9, 19-33).

In chapter 17, Jesus talks about uppity servants who come into the house after plowing or keeping sheep and expect the owner of the farm to prepare a hot meal for them. Jesus asks whether the owner would not say to the servants, "Prepare supper for me, put on your apron and serve me while I eat and drink; later you may eat and drink" (7-10). Jesus speaks, we suspect, about those of us who forget our station with God and expect him to treat us more royally than we deserve.

In chapter 19 is the story of the pounds, known in Matthew's Gospel as the parable of the talents (Matthew 25:14-30). A nobleman takes a long journey, and while he is away, he entrusts ten servants with a pound apiece, saying, "Do business with these until I come back." When he returns, he calls in the servants to see what they have done with his money. One has turned the single pound into ten, and is praised. Another has turned the pound into five, and is likewise commended. But one of the ten has done nothing with his pound but hide it in a napkin, and the master is so angry that he takes the pound away from him and gives it to the man who turned his pound into ten (Luke 19:11-27).

Finally, after the story of the vineyard in chapter 20, there is an unexpected positive note—I say "unexpected," for all the other examples have been negative. In chapter 21, Jesus was sitting by the temple treasury, watching people bring their gifts, when he was struck by the sight of a widow putting in two copper coins. "Truly I tell you," he said to the disciples, "this poor widow has put in more than all of them; for all of them have contributed out of their abundance, but she out of her poverty put in all she had to live on" (Luke 21:1-4).

The story of the vineyard, you see, was no passing thought with Jesus, and it probably was not intended to speak of Israel alone. Everywhere he looked, Jesus saw people who were greedy, selfish, and avaricious, people who forgot that God owns the world, that all of us are his servants, who should live sensitively, caringly, and generously with all his other servants.

Mixed-up Priorities

Jesus would see the same thing today, wouldn't he, if he were to walk in our midst? He would see people who think their nice houses and automobiles belong to them; who believe their jewelry and bank accounts and CDs are theirs alone; who forget that their stocks and bonds, their investments in businesses and apartment houses, are really God's, not their own; who live without concern for the poor and hungry or for the victims of war in small countries on the other side of the globe; who turn a blind eye to the way we are despoiling the lakes and seas and polluting the atmosphere, without remembering that they are a trust from God for future generations.

What failures we are as royal custodians!

We erect beautiful homes for ourselves and curse the government when it erects hovels for the poor.

We pay astronomical salaries to TV stars, athletes, and executives, and almost nothing to those who teach our children.

We indulge ourselves in $30 meals and $500 suits and $25,000 automobiles, and give $5 a week to the church.

We spend millions on banks and insurance companies and corporation headquarters, and make the churches and colleges and charitable organizations beg for a pittance.

It's all backward, isn't it? Our priorities are turned upside down; the scale of values is confused.

Archbishop William Temple once said that it's as if a prankster had slipped into the store window at night and mixed up all the pricetags, so that a pair of roller skates costs $5,000 and a fur coat is only $1.98. Having forgotten that the earth is the Lord's, and the fullness thereof, we don't know what is worth what. We teach our children to work sixty hours a week for financial security and prestige in the community, and we don't care if they forget how to be loving and tender toward one another. We erect enormous buildings for our financial and scientific institutions, while we permit many churches and synagogues to fall to rack and ruin for lack of funds. We say we believe in God, but many of the things we do proclaim our belief in earthly security and self-indulgence.

Living as Proper Tenants

"Do not store up for yourselves treasures on earth," said Jesus, "where moth and rust consume and where thieves break in and steal; but store up for yourselves treasures in heaven, where neither moth nor rust consumes and where thieves do not break in and steal. For where your treasure is, there your heart will be also" (Matthew 6:19-21).

That's the secret, isn't it? Where the treasure is, the heart follows. If our treasure is in earthly things, our hearts are imprisoned in the earth, and we forget our custodianship, we forget that the whole earth belongs to God. It is when we remember *whose* we are and *whose* the earth is that our hearts are able to soar and life becomes truly beautiful.

Wouldn't it be wonderful if nothing in the earth belonged to anyone who did not remember that it is God's and use it accordingly? It would solve all our problems of property ownership, food distribution, medical help, and education for the masses. If only nothing belonged to anyone who did not acknowledge God's true ownership, our world would function as a paradise!

Jesus knew the world would never work this way, not short of some apocalyptic reversal, at any rate; but he did require of his followers that they—*we*—behave as if everything belongs to God. We are not responsible for the actions of the rest of the people of the world, only for our own. We are to remember *our* custodianship and to live as proper tenants, giving glory to the real owner of everything.

Handling Everything as if It Were God's

A friend told me about a minister who was visited by a young couple whose aunt had recently died. When the aunt's will was read, the couple learned they had inherited $1.5 million. They were stunned, for they had no idea the aunt had so much money.

"This fortune is destroying us," they said to the minister. "We used to enjoy life enormously. We are simple people with simple tastes. Now we have all this money, and it's worrying us to death. What should we do with it?"

"Give it away," said the minister.

"But we can't do that," said the couple.

"You said it's destroying you. You should give it away." So they agreed to go and pray about it.

A week later, they went to the minister and said, "You're right. We have prayed about the money and we have decided to give it away. We have drawn up a list of worthy causes we would consider giving it to, and we would like you to look over the list and give us your opinion."

The minister took the list and looked at it. "These are all wonderful causes," he said. "I know most of them and think quite highly of them. But you should keep the money."

"What was that?" they asked.

"I said, 'You should keep the money.' "

"But you said we should give it away."

"Ah, yes," said the minister, "that was when you thought the money was yours. Now that you know it isn't, you should keep it and use it. If you give it all away, it will help the recipients right now. But if you take care of it and act as stewards of it for God, it will go much further and bless more people in the long run."

The person who told me this story said, "I am telling you this because it has changed my life. I now understand what it means to be a steward of the things that belong to God. It means that I am responsible for them all the time. I can't merely give them away and be done with it. I have to handle everything every day as if it is God's."

"Handle everything every day as if it is God's." That's what Jesus was trying to teach his disciples. It is what he would like to teach us. And if we learn it, we will be like the prudent servant in the parable who heard his master say, "Well done, good and faithful servant; you have been faithful over a little, I will set you over much; enter into the joy of your master" (Matthew 25:21, 23 RSV).

John Killinger

TEMPERANCE AND PATIENCE

But knowledge is not the end of the work of grace. To it we must add *temperance*. Without it, both faith and reason may soon relinquish their rightful place to temporal pleasures. Temperance is an excellent steward. It regularly inspects the soul and sets the saint's affections in order so that he does not ignore holy duties to pursue his own entertainment. If you allow your love of creature comforts—or even your pleasure in family and loved ones—to outrun your love for the Lord, you cannot be a victorious soldier for Christ. Therefore, pray for temperance, which keeps the spiritual gauge of your heart well within the safety range.

Imagine yourself now well equipped and marching toward heaven while basking in prosperity. Should you not also prepare for foul weather—i.e., a period of adversity? Satan will line the hedges with a thousand temptations when you come into the narrow lanes of adversity, where you cannot run as in the day of your prosperity. You may manage to escape an alluring world, only to be flattened when trouble strikes, unless you know how to persevere. Therefore, the apostle commands, "to temperance [add] *patience*" (2 Peter 1:6).

Do you have patience? An excellent grace indeed, but not enough. You must be pious as well. So Peter continues, "to patience [add] *godliness*" (v. 6). Godliness encompasses the whole worship of God, inward and outward. Your morals may be impeccable, but if you do not worship God, then you are an atheist. If you worship Him and that devoutly, but not according to Scripture, you are an idolater. If according to the rule, but not according to the spirit of the Gospel, then you are a hypocrite. The only worship that leads to the inner chamber of true godliness is that which is done "in spirit and in truth" (John 4:24).

William Gurnall

LAYING OUR BURDEN DOWN

Most Christians are like a man who was toiling along the road, bending under a heavy burden, when a wagon overtook him, and the driver kindly offered to help him on his journey. He joyfully accepted the offer, but when seated, continued to bend beneath his burden, which he still kept on his shoulders. "Why do you not lay down your burden?" asked the kind-hearted driver. "Oh!" replied the man, "I feel that it is almost too much to ask you to carry me, and I could not think of letting you carry my burden too." And so Christians, who have given themselves into the care and keeping of the Lord Jesus, still continue to bend beneath the weight of their burden, and often go weary and heavy-laden throughout the whole length of their journey.

When I speak of burdens, I mean everything that troubles us, whether spiritual or temporal.

I mean, first of all, ourselves. The greatest burden we have to carry in life is self. The most difficult thing we have to manage is self. Our own daily living, our frames and feelings, our especial weaknesses and temptations, . . . these are the things that perplex and worry us more than anything else, and that bring us oftenest into bondage and darkness. In laying off your burdens, therefore, the first one you must get rid of is yourself. . . .

Next, you must lay off every other burden—your health, your reputation, your Christian work, your houses, your children, your business, your servants; everything, in short, that concerns you, whether inward or outward. . . .

I knew a Christian lady who had a very heavy temporal burden. It took away her sleep and her appetite, and there was danger of her health breaking down under it. . . . The circumstances of her life she could not alter, but she took them to the Lord, and handed them over into His management; and then she believed that He took it, and she left all the responsibility and the worry and anxiety with Him. . . . She abandoned her whole self to the Lord, with all that she was and all that she had, and, believing that He took that which she had committed to Him, she ceased to fret and worry, and her life became all sunshine in the gladness of belonging to Him. And this was the Higher Christian Life! . . .

Would you like to get rid of your burdens? Do you not long to hand over the management of your unmanageable self into the hands of One who is able to manage you? Are you not tired and weary, and does not the rest I speak of look sweet to you? . . .

Your part is simply to rest. His part is to sustain you, and He cannot fail.

Hannah Whitall Smith
1832–1911

HUMILITY

Humility is the great ornament and jewel of the Christian religion, . . . first put into a discipline and made a part of a religion by our Lord Jesus Christ. . . .

For all the world, all that we are, and all that we have, our bodies and our souls, our actions and our sufferings, our conditions at home, our accidents [or experiences] abroad, our many sins and our seldom virtues, are as so many arguments to make our souls dwell low in the deep valleys of humility. . . .

The humble man . . . does not . . . pursue the choice of his own will, but in all things lets God choose for him and his superiors in those things which concern them. He does not murmur against commands. . . . He patiently bears injuries. He is always unsatisfied in his own conduct, resolutions, and counsels. He is a great lover of good men, and praiser of wise men, and a censurer of no man. He is modest in his speech, and reserved in his laughter. He fears when he hears himself commended, lest God make another judgment concerning his actions than men do. . . . He mends his faults, and gives thanks, when he is admonished.

The grace of humility is exercised by these following rules:

Love to be concealed, and little esteemed: be content to want [or lack] praise, never being troubled when thou art slighted or undervalued; for thou canst not undervalue thyself, and if thou thinkest so meanly as there is reason, no contempt will seem unreasonable, and therefore it will be very tolerable.

Never speak anything directly to thy praise or glory; that is, with purpose to be commended, and for no other end.

When thou hast said or done a thing for which thou receivest praise or estimation, take it indifferently, and return it to God, reflecting upon him as the giver of the gift, or the blesser of the action, . . . and give God thanks for making thee an instrument of his glory, for the benefit of others.

Secure a good name to thyself by living virtuously and humbly; but let this good name be nursed abroad, and never be brought home to look upon it. . . .

Use no stratagems and devices to get praise. Some used to inquire into the faults of their own actions or discourses on purpose to hear that it was well done or spoken and without fault. . . .

Suffer [or permit] others to be praised in thy presence, and entertain their good and glory with delight; but at no hand disparage them, or lessen the report, or make an objection; and think not the advancement of thy brother is a lessening of thy worth. . . .

Never compare thyself with others, unless it be to advance them and to depress thyself. . . .

Remember that the blessed Savior of the world hath done more to prescribe, and transmit, and secure this grace, than any other; his whole life being a great continued example of humility, a vast descent from the glorious bosom of His Father, to the womb of a poor maiden, to the form of a servant, to the miseries of a sinner, to a life of labor, to a state of poverty, to a death of malefactors, to the grave of death, and to the intolerable calamities which we deserved. . . .

Jeremy Taylor
1613–1667

THE DISCONTENTED TAILOR

It is a wise man who knows when he has enough. The effort to get more may result in misfortune and misery.

A tailor and a goldsmith were walking one evening through the woods and wondering if they should ever be rich men with gold to spare. They heard the sound of distant music and went to see what caused it.

The moon had risen, and on a little hillock they saw a band of tiny men dancing in a ring with hands joined, while an old man, with hair down to his waist, played on a pipe. This made the music which the tailor and goldsmith had heard.

They stopped and watched the dancers for a while. At last the old man beckoned them to join the circle and dance with the tiny men. Seeing how many they were, the tailor and the goldsmith agreed and soon were dancing as merrily as the best of them.

Then the old man took a pair of shears and cut off all the hair and beard of the tailor and the goldsmith until they were quite bald. This made the tiny men laugh, and they were merrier than ever.

Then all at once every one began to gather rocks and fill his pockets full. The goldsmith and the tailor did likewise, and then when the moon went down they all lay down and went fast to sleep.

What do you think? In the morning when the tailor and the goldsmith woke their hair and their beard had grown again, and the rocks had turned to gold in their pockets.

"Oh, this is plenty for me," cried the goldsmith. "I shall now live in ease the rest of my life. I shall build me a house, and get me a wife and buy a horse and carriage. Oh, I have enough for my purposes!"

The tailor looked at his gold, and though he had never lived in anything but a room back of his shop, yet he said:

"This is not enough for me. I want a palace and many servants, and a whole troop of horses. I shall go back to the tiny men to-night." So he hid his gold in a tree and waited for the night to come.

The goldsmith went on home, but the tailor waited until the moon had risen and then joined the tiny men in their dance. He could hardly wait for the old man to cut off his hair and beard. He took the shears and cut it himself. Then when the time came to gather rocks he eagerly filled his pockets, his shoes, his hat and held some in his hands.

"I may as well get a plenty," said he.

Then they all lay down and went to sleep. Early the tailor woke up and felt for his rocks. They were still hard rocks. When he hunted for his gold of the night before, it also had turned back to rocks. Besides that, his hair and beard had not grown out, and he was quite bald. The poor tailor had lost what he had because he was not satisfied with enough.

Lowton B. Evans

THE BLASTED PINE

Far away, in the gloomy old forests of Maine,
Towered aloft, in his pride, a dark evergreen pine,
And he said, looking down on the lowlier trees,
"None hath strength, or endurance, or beauty, like mine."

Ere the boast was well spoken, the sunlight had fled,
And the storm cloud was bursting in wrath o'er his head;
From its bosom the bolt of Jehovah was thrown,
And the pride of the forest lay riven and prone.

"Why art thou here, my old friend?" said an oak, at whose foot,
The proud boaster, rebuked, was now helplessly laid;
Of his strength and endurance no traces remained;
Of his beauty—the wreck which the lightening had made.

Thus the pine meekly replied: "I forgot my birth,
And rejoiced in o'ertopping my brothers on earth;
Now all broken and weak, on her bosom I lie,
Unavailing to mourn, and neglected to die"

MORAL
If the story be simple, the moral is plain—
Who *exalteth* himself, shall be *humbled* again.

THE POT OF GOLD

Chrif Begins the Search

Once upon a time there stood by the roadside an old red house. In this house lived three people. They were an old grandmother; her grandchild, Rhoda; and a boy named Christopher. Christopher was no relation to Rhoda and her grandmother. He was called Chrif for short.

The grandmother earned her living by picking berries. Every day in fair weather she went to the pastures. But she did not take the children with her. They played at home.

Rhoda had a flower garden in an old boat. The boat was filled with earth. There grew larkspur and sweet-william. Rhoda loved her flowers and tended them faithfully.

Chrif did not care much for flowers. He preferred to sail boats. He would cut them out of wood with his jack-knife, and load them with stones and grass. Then he would send the boats down the little stream that flowed past the old red house.

"This ship is going to India," he would say to Rhoda. "She carries gold and will bring back pearls and rice."

"How much you know, Chrif," said Rhoda.

"I mean to go to India some day," said Chrif. "People ride on elephants there."

Rhoda would sail little twigs in the stream. Her boats were small, but they sometimes went farther than Chrif's. His were loaded so heavily, that they often overturned.

One day the children were sailing boats when a thunder-storm arose. How fast the rain fell! And how fast they ran to the house!

"Poor grandmother will be all wet!" said Rhoda. She and Chrif were watching the falling rain from the window.

Suddenly the sun came out. A little rain was still falling, but the children ran into the yard.

"Look, there's a rainbow!" cried Chrif. "What pretty colors! And how ugly our old red house looks! I wish I were where the rainbow is."

"I see just the color of my larkspur in the rainbow," said Rhoda.

"O pooh!" said Chrif, "only a flower! That's not much. Now if

I were only rich, I wouldn't stay here. I'd go off into the world. How grand it must be over there beyond the rainbow."

"One end is quite near us," said Rhoda.

"Are ye looking for a pot of gold, children?" said a voice behind them. It was the old broom-woman. She had a little house in the woods and sold brooms for a living.

"A pot of gold!" cried Chrif. "Where is it?"

"It's at the foot of the rainbow," said the broom-woman. "If ye get to the foot of the rainbow and then dig and dig, ye'll come to a pot of gold."

"Rhoda! Let's go quick!" said Chrif.

"No," said Rhoda, "I ought to weed my flowers."

"Ye must hurry," laughed the old broom-woman. "The rainbow won't stay for lazy folks."

"I'm off!" cried Chrif; and away he went in search of the pot of gold. Rhoda watched him out of sight. Then she turned to weed the boat-garden.

When her grandmother came from the berry pasture, Rhoda told her where Chrif had gone. "We shall all be rich when he comes back with his pot of gold," said the little girl.

"He will not find it," said the grandmother. Rhoda, however, was not so sure.

Chrif in the New Land

Chrif ran straight across the fields toward the glowing rainbow. One end of the lovely arch seemed to touch the top of a distant hill. Chrif climbed the hill, but the rainbow was no longer there. It rested on the far side of a valley. Chrif hurried down the hill and into the valley. When he reached the spot where the end of the rainbow had rested, the rainbow was gone. Chrif could see it nowhere.

The lad stopped and looked around him. Not far away a flock of sheep were feeding. A shepherd-boy lay on the ground near them. He was reading a book.

Chrif crept to the shepherd-boy's side and read over his shoulder. This is what he read: "Beyond the setting of the sun lies the New Land. Here are mountains, forests, and mighty rivers. The sands of the streams are golden; the trees grow wonderful fruit; the mountains hide strange monsters. Upon a high pillar near the coast is the famous pot of gold."

"Oh, where is this country?" cried Chrif.

"Will you go?" asked Gavin, the shepherd-boy.

"Go! That I will," said Chrif. "The pot of gold is there, and that is what I have set out to find."

"Yes," said Gavin, "the pot of gold is there and many other things. I long to see them all. Let us hurry on our way."

The two boys first went through a forest. Then they came out upon the ocean side. The sun was setting in the sea. A path of gold lay across the water.

A ship was about to set sail. Her white canvas was spread; her oars were in place. Her deck was crowded with boys. They were all starting for the wonderful New Land across the sea.

Chrif and Gavin climbed on board and the ship bounded from the land.

On and on they went, straight into the sunset. The rowers sang as they worked. Gavin tried to read his book, but Chrif looked eagerly ahead. How he longed to see the new country to which they were going!

And very soon the New Land came in sight. Then a party landed; Chrif, Gavin, and a boy named Andy were among them.

They walked some distance and then night darkened down around them. The mountains looked cruel; the fields barren. "Let us return to the ship," said many.

But Chrif would not turn back. "I must find the pot of gold," he said, "it cannot now be far away." And Gavin and Andy went with him.

"I should like to dip my fingers into your pot of gold," said Andy.

"You shall have your share," said Chrif. "It is on the top of a pillar not far from the coast. If you'll stand below, I'll get on your shoulders, and then perhaps I can reach it."

"Only don't let it drop on my head," said Andy, with a laugh.

They walked along the shore in silence. After a time Chrif cried out with joy. "Here is a path leading into the woods. And I do believe I see the pillar!"

"Hurrah!" cried Andy, "let's push on!"

And now the three stood at the foot of the pillar and looked up to the top. By the faint light of the moon they saw the pot of gold.

"Climb on Andy's shoulders, Gavin, and then I will stand on yours," said Chrif.

"I don't want the pot of gold," said Gavin. "I have seen it; that is enough. I will go to see the Magic Fountain," and Gavin turned into the forest.

The other two friends stood by the pillar. "I must have that pot of gold. I want it for Rhoda and the old grandmother."

As Chrif spoke, he looked at the pillar. Lo! A picture was on its side. He saw the old red house, the grandmother at the window, and Rhoda in the garden. Rhoda was watering the flowers in the dear old boat. Now and then she would turn her head and look up the road. She seemed hoping that Chrif would come.

The pillar and the pot of gold faded away; then the picture of home went too. Chrif was left in darkness.

Then Andy spoke. "Hark!" he whispered, "I hear something."

Chrif at the Palace

Chrif listened and he too heard distant music. Its notes were very sweet.

"Come, let us go where the music is!" said Andy.

Chrif and Andy made their way through the woods and entered a shining city. Every street was blazing with lights; the fronts of the houses were hung with lanterns; fireworks were being set off in the public squares. All the people wore their finest clothes.

"How happy they all are! I wonder why?" said Andy.

"Hush!" cried Chrif.

A man on a prancing horse had just come in sight. He reined in his horse and blew a horn. Then he cried with a loud voice these words: "This night there is a ball in the palace. All are welcome. The Pot of Gold will be given to the one with whom the Princess shall dance."

"Hurrah!" cried the people. "Hurrah! Hurrah!" cried Chrif, louder than them all.

When Chrif and Andy entered the palace, they saw the Princess upon her throne. Dancing was going on, but the Princess did not dance. She was waiting for the handsomest dancer. All who thought themselves good looking stood in a row not far from the Princess. Each lad was trying to look handsomer than the others in the line.

Over the throne was a pearl clock. It was that kind of clock called a cuckoo clock. When the hours struck, a golden cuckoo would come out of a little door. Then he would cuckoo as many times as there were hours and then go back, shutting the door after him.

When Chrif and Andy entered the hall, the Princess saw them at once. "Those two are the handsomest of all," she thought, "and one of them is handsomer than the other."

She looked at Chrif again. Then she stepped down from the throne.

"Dance with me," she said, "and you shall have the pot of gold," and she held out her hand to Chrif.

"What was I to do with it?" asked Chrif. "Oh, I know. I was to take it home to Rhoda."

That moment the little bird burst open the little pearl door. "Cuckoo! cuckoo! cockoo!" he cried.

But to Chrif he seemed to say: "Rhoda sits by the window watching for Chrif. The flowers are dead in the boat-garden. 'Chrif will never come back,' says grandmother, 'he cares nothing for us.'"

Again Chrif saw the beautiful hall and the Princess standing before him. Then, suddenly, the music grew harsh; the palace walls fell; the dancers were gone. Chrif was all alone.

Chrif and His Books

When day dawned, Chrif was walking over a wide plain. On the far side of the plain stood a ruined house. Between a row of poplar trees a path led to the door.

Chrif knocked, but no one came. Then he pushed open the door and entered. An old man sat at a table. The table was covered with great books and many papers. Overhead a lamp burned dimly.

The old man was bent over the books. He seemed to study busily, but when Chrif went near, he saw that the old man was dead.

There were two doors to this room. One was the door by which Chrif had entered. The other was opposite. This door was of stone. On it was written: "Behind this door is the Pot of Gold. To open you must first read the words written below."

The words written below were strange; the letters too were strange.

"These books may help me read the writing," thought Chrif. "This old man has spent his life in the search. Shall I be more successful I wonder?"

Then he buried the old man, lighted the lamp, and read the books. Weeks passed and even months. Chrif ate little and slept less.

At last, one day, he lifted a shining face. "I have found the secret!" he cried, "the letters are plain."

Then stepping to the door, he read: "Knock and this door will open."

Chrif knocked once, and the door flew open. One shining spot he saw in the darkness. It was the pot of gold.

Chrif put out his hand to take it, when lo! burning words shone on its side. And Chrif read: —

"I am the Pot of Gold; I can give thee all things save one. If thou hast me, thou canst not have that. Close thine eyes. Then, if thou choosest me, open them again."

Chrif closed his eyes. He saw the old red house dark and cold. No one lived there now. The boat-garden was hidden under the snow. Some one in white passed him by. She was weeping bitterly. "Rhoda!" he cried and followed in her steps.

Suddenly a warm hand fell upon his shoulder.

"Chrif, dear Chrif!"

He opened his eyes, and O joy! Rhoda stood beside him.

Chrif's Return

"I have come to look for you," said Rhoda. "Why, Chrif, you have been gone three years!"

"Three years!" gasped Chrif.

"When grandmother died, last winter, I was so lonely, I said, 'When spring comes I will find Chrif.' "

"Grandmother dead! Why, it was but yesterday that I left home!"

"Ah, no," answered Rhoda. And she looked at Chrif and smiled.

And so they came again to the old red house. There was the dear old boat-garden. Sweetpeas were in bloom and morning-glories climbed up the side of the house. It was very pleasant.

As they stood by the boat-garden, a voice called to them. The old broom-woman stood in the road.

"Have ye found the pot of gold?" she asked.

"No, but I have found something else far better!" said Chrif, "I have found home."

Fannie E. Coe

HOFUS THE STONECUTTER

Once upon a time in Japan, there was a poor stone-cutter, named Hofus, who used to go every day to the mountain-side to cut great blocks of stone. He lived near the mountain in a little stone hut, and worked hard and was happy.

One day he took a load of stone to the house of a rich man. There he saw so many beautiful things that when he went back to his mountain he could think of nothing else. Then he began to wish that he too might sleep in a bed as soft as down, with curtains of silk, and tassels of gold. And he sighed:

> Ah me! Ah me!
> If Hofus only were rich as he!

To his surprise, the voice of the Mountain Spirit answered:

> Have thou thy wish!

When Hofus returned home that evening his little hut was gone, and in its place stood a great palace. It was filled with beautiful things, and the best of all was a bed of down, with curtains of silk and tassels of gold.

Hofus decided to work no more. But he was not used to being idle, and time passed slowly,—the days seemed very long.

One day as he sat by the window he saw a carriage dash past. It was drawn by snow-white horses. In it sat a prince, while before and behind were servants in suits of blue and white. One was holding a golden umbrella over the prince.

When the stone-cutter saw this, he began to feel unhappy, and he sighed:

> Ah me! Ah me!
> If Hofus only a prince might be!

And again the same voice that he had heard on the mountain answered:

> Be thou a prince!

Straightway Hofus was a prince. He had servants dressed in crimson and gold, and he rode in a carriage with a golden umbrella over his head.

For a short time he was happy, but one day, as he walked in the garden, he saw that the flowers were drooping, the grass was dry and brown. And when he rode out he felt the hot sun burn him in spite of his umbrella.

"The sun is mightier than I," thought he, and then he sighed:

> Ah me! Ah me!
> If Hofus only the sun might be!

And the voice answered:

> Be thou the sun!

Straightway the great sun he became. He burned the grass and rice-fields, he dried up the streams. Rich and poor alike suffered from the terrible heat.

One day a cloud came and rested in front of him, and hid the earth from his sight. He was angry and cried:

> Ah me! Ah me!
> If Hofus only a cloud might be!

And the voice answered: —

> Be thou a cloud!

Straightway a cloud he became. He floated before the face of the sun, and hid the earth from it.

Then day after day the cloud dropped rain. The rivers overflowed, and the rice-fields were covered with water. Towns were swept away. Only the great rocks on the mountain-side stood unmoved midst the flood.

The cloud looked at them in wonder, then he sighed: —

Ah me! Ah me!
If Hofus only a rock might be!

And the voice answered:—

Be thou a rock!

Straightway a rock he became. Proudly he stood. The sun could not burn him and the rain could not move him.

"Now, at last," he said, "no one is mightier than I."

But one day he was waked from his dreams by a noise,—tap! tap! tap!—down at his feet. He looked and there was a stone-cutter driving his tool into the rock. Another blow and the great rock shivered; a block of stone broke away.

"That man is mightier than I!" cried Hofus, and he sighed:—

Ah me! Ah me!
If Hofus only the man might be!

And the voice answered:—

Be thou thyself!

And straightaway Hofus was himself again,—a poor stone-cutter, working all day upon the mountain-side, and going home at night to his little hut. But he was content and happy, and never again did he wish to be other than Hofus the stone-cutter.

A Japanese Legend

FORTITUDE

Having fortitude means having courage, but it means much more. To have courage means to be strong and to stand up for what we believe is right. It may be easy to take a stand against some great evil, but with fortitude, we not only take bold action of the sake of the Kingdom, but we may daily endure slights, and even pain and suffering. Fortitude also mean responsibility. God expects us to take care of the earth and of all creation. Sometimes this means working. Our work may be very simple or it may be very hard, but God always expects us to do our very best. Sometimes fortitude means choosing to do the right things, by sticking with our work or our friends when it would be easier to quit.

May you be made strong with all the strength that comes from his glorious power, and may you be prepared to endure everything with patience.
Colossians 1:11 NRSV

I AM PERSUADED

Who shall separate us from the love of Christ? shall tribulation, or distress, or persecution, or famine, or nakedness, or peril, or word?

As it is written, For thy sake we are killed all the day long; we are accounted as sheep for the slaughter.

Nay, in all things we are more than conquerors through him that loved us.

For I am persuaded, that neither death, nor life, nor angels, nor principalities, nor powers, nor things present, nor things to come,

Nor height, nor depth, nor any other creature, shall be able to separate us from the love of God, which is in Christ Jesus our Lord.

Romans 9:35-39 KJV

PATIENCE IN SUFFERING

Be patient, therefore, beloved, until the coming of the Lord. The farmer waits for the precious crop from the earth, being patient with it until it receives the early and the later rains. You also must be patient. Strengthen your hearts, for the coming of the Lord is near. Beloved, do not grumble against one another, so that you may not be judged. See, the Judge is standing at the doors! As an example of suffering and patience, beloved, take the prophets who spoke in the name of the Lord. Indeed we call blessed those who showed endurance. You have heard of the endurance of Job, and you have seen the purpose of the Lord, how the Lord is compassionate and merciful.

James 5:7-11 NRSV

PERSEVERANCE

As a young physician attempting to become a novelist, A. J. Cronin retreated to the Scottish highlands for the calm surroundings many writers require. After three months, an effort he deemed unworthy was thrown in the trash, and he walked out into the countryside, frustrated and dejected.

He happened upon a farmer ditching a bog, in the hope of converting it to pasture land. The old farmer knew of the writer's fruitless labors, and after a time, he spoke:

> My father ditched this bog . . . and never made a pasture. I've dug it all my days, and I've never made a pasture. But . . . I cannot help but dig. For my father knew, and I know, that if you only dig enough, a pasture can be made here.

Cronin understood the message, and eventually he became a renowned writer.

Job's virtue was not so much patience as perseverance. Inquiring, exploring—frustrated, he persevered. Dig and dig some more, until the treasure of the Kingdom is found.

Barry Culbertson

THE SERMON IN THE WILDERNESS

"My friend, I have explained that I must have the horse, and that I will deposit with thee his full value until his safe return within a week's time."

The tall man spoke a trifle wearily, as though he had had almost enough of the argument. It was a hot day on the edge of the great Pennsylvania forest. The dust in front of the Rockville tavern still hung in a cloud where the coach, on its weekly arrival from the distant city, had stirred it a-fresh. The group of farmers, waiting for mail and news of the outside world, had watched with curious eyes this stranger descend from the high seat beside the driver. They had noted the broad-brimmed hat, white stock, carpet bag and closely fitting "store" clothes that marked him as city-bred, and the foreign way he used his hands when he talked. Their natural distrust had melted, however, before the radiant smile of more than ordinary good-will that lighted up the blue eyes and wrinkled the lean face as he strode briskly toward them crying, "The peace of God be with you, my friends! From which of you may I obtain a horse for a journey into the wilderness!"

Several minutes of parley followed between the innkeeper and the stranger, not a word being lost by the eager group of listeners. This man insisted that he must travel for three days straight into the heart of the forest "along a way that would be opened" to him. The innkeeper objected that there was only one trail a horse could travel, and this exceedingly dangerous, with treacherous fords and rocky pitfalls. Did the stranger know that the three-days' trail led only to a lumber camp, and that honest men who valued their lives or their purses did well to avoid this place? Adventurous explorers had been known to enter the dark forest, never to return. Was the gentleman's business so imperative that he would risk his life?

"It is my Father's business, and the most imperative in the world," answered the stranger calmly. "Should a hundred men beset my path, I should go on unharmed. I have received my instructions from Above and go without fear, for the Spirit upholds me. So, if I may hire a horse of thee —"

At length a wiry little mare was brought out and a dozen hands helped saddle her. The stranger, though urged to remain over night, refused courteously, explaining that he carried food and was accustomed to sleep in the open. As he paid for the mare and was about to ride away, the innkeeper inquired, "What is your name, stranger!"

"Stephen Grellet, of New York, and I go to carry the message of God to those who will listen."

As the little mare and the man climbed the rough path and disappeared into the birches that edged the dark pines, one man remarked, "A Quaker, I know by his speech, and a godly man. But he cannot melt the hearts of those men with his soft tongue."

Stephen Grellet found a single trail winding now along the slippery banks of a rushing stream, now over treacherous moss-covered rocks, skirting steep cliffs, and twice plunging through the river where the mare was forced to swim. During the first afternoon he passed several clearings with little cabins, where children ran out to wave and call to him; but after this he saw no work of human hands except the logs left by receding spring floods along the banks. Though no sounds except those of the forest came to his ears, he moved with a radiance in his eyes and with a smile upon his lips, as though he were listening to the cheery words of a dear companion.

Early in the afternoon of the third day—a breathless day, when even the birds were voiceless and the low, pulsing drone of insects made the silence seem only more profound—Stephen Grellet found the trail widened into a corduroy road where horses had evidently been used to drag the logs down to the river bank. He noticed a pile of rusty cans and a piece of chain hanging on a branch. Then rounding a huge rock, Stephen suddenly found himself on the edge of a space from which all trees and underbrush had been cleared. Facing him on the far side stood a large three-sided log shed; to the left and right of this shed were several rough, closed cabins, the bark from their slab sides hanging in tatters. A pile of black embers in the center of the space added a last touch of desolation.

Stephen Grellet reined in his mare in great perplexity. The

message that had come to him had been very clear, and as was the habit of his life, he had followed the leading of the Spirit in perfect faith. He knew that he was to come to this spot in the heart of the wilderness where a gang of woodcutters, far-famed for their lawlessness, had been operating, and here he was to preach the simple and holy truth of God's presence in the forest. It had not once occurred to him that, as evidently was the case, the lumbermen might have moved on deeper into the forest. He knew without question, however, that this was the place where he must preach. Alighting, he tied his mare to a sapling, leaving her to browse the long wood grass, and made his way to the central cabin where rough tables stood on a slightly raised floor. Mounting this platform, he faced the forest, a strange inner light making his face glow. During his long life he had traveled to the far corners of the earth, defying dangers and discomforts in order to carry the simple assurance of God's love to all people; yet never had he felt more completely the Divine Presence flooding through and around his whole being than when now he stood alone in the deserted camp, surrounded by the mystery of the forest. The afternoon sun, slanting between the brown tree pillars, fell upon a gold-green mass of ferns at his feet, and the fronds quivered, stirred by some tiny wood beast scampering through the stems.

"Oh, God—thou art here—here!" he cried, stretching wide his arms. As if in answer, a low murmur breathed in the tree-tops, swelling nearer, moving the pine needles softly. Then a loud rustle, perhaps of a startled animal behind the cabin, gave Stephen Grellet the sense that all around him were the invisible eyes and ears of the forest folk. To them and to God he spoke aloud, his words, blending the faith and joy of his own soul with the dignity of the pines, the grace of the fern fronds, the vitality of the little scurrying beasts, and over all the softly moving Presence in the wind-stirred branches.

At last, silent, with head bowed, he heard far off the leisurely, bell-like notes of the thrush thrilling through the forest spaces. With infinite peace in his heart he mounted the little mare and rode away, back to Rockville and the world.

Six years later Stephen Grellet was in London. He had gone there, as he had gone into the forests of Pennsylvania, guided only by the Spirit. He had gone down into the narrow, filthy streets, where men and women seemed too sodden to understand when he told them of the love of the Father, and he had preached in dark prisons where men looked at him dully when he spoke of the Divine Light. Yet whenever he ceased speaking there were always some who crowded nearer, seeking to know more of this Being who had sent him to show them the way out of their wretchedness.

Late one afternoon, smothered by the stagnant air of the slums, he walked on London Bridge as the setting sun was throwing a broken red path on the oily water of the Thames. He was very tired, for he threw all his strength into the struggle to show to others the Light that burned in his own soul. As he stood looking at the spires of the vast city against the glow of the evening sky, he prayed for faith and peace. Suddenly the roar of London died in his ears and he heard again the gentle sighing of the pines in the Pennsylvania forest and the clear notes of the thrush. Just as truly God was with him here—

The revery of Stephen Grellet was shattered by someone seizing him roughly by the elbow. He turned quickly to face a broad, muscular man, with rugged face and eyes of piercing eagerness, who cried, in great excitement, as he peered into Stephen Grellet's face, "I have got you at last! I have got you at last!"

Stephen returned the gaze calmly, but could see nothing familiar about the man except that he was certainly an American.

"Friend," he replied, "I think thou art mistaken."

"But I am not—I cannot be! I have carried every line of your face in my memory for six years. How I have longed to see it again!"

"Who, then, art thou, and where dost thou think we have met?" inquired Stephen.

"Did you not preach in the great forest in Pennsylvania, three days' trip from the village of Rockville, six years ago last midsummer?"

"I did, but I saw no one there to listen."

The man held out his hands to Stephen Grellet—strong hands that had known hard toil. "I was there," he replied, his voice full of awe as the memory rose again before him. "I was the head of the woodmen who had deserted those shanties. We had moved on into the forest and were putting up more cabins to live in, when I discovered that I had left my lever at the old settlement. So, leaving my men at work, I went back alone for my tool. As I approached the old place I heard a voice. Trembling and agitated, I drew near, and saw you through the chinks in the timber walls of our dining shanty. I listened to you, and something in your face or in your words, or both, stirred me as I had never been stirred before. I went back to my men. I was miserable for weeks; I had no Bible, no book of any kind, no one to speak to about divine things.

"At last I found the strength I needed. I obtained a Bible; I told my men the blessed news that God was near us, and we learned together to ask forgiveness and to lead better lives. Three of us became missionaries and went forth to tell thousands of others of the joy and faith you brought into the forest."

From THE CHILDREN'S STORY GARDEN
Collected by a Committee of the Philadelphia
Yearly Meeting of Friends. © *1920*
by J. B. Lippincott Company.

O Word of God Incarnate

O Word of God incarnate,
O Wisdom from on high,
O Truth unchanged, unchanging,
O Light of our dark sky:
We praise thee for the radiance
That from the hallowed page,
A lantern to our footsteps,
Shines on from age to age.

The Church from her dear Master
Received the gift divine,
And still that light she lifteth
O'er all the earth to shine.
It is the golden casket
Where gems of truth are stored;
It is the heaven-drawn picture
Of Christ, the living Word.

It floateth like a banner
Before God's host unfurled;
It shineth like a beacon
Above the darkling world;
It is the chart and compass
That o'er life's surging sea,
Mid rocks and mists and quicksands,
Still guides, O Christ, to Thee.

William W. How
1867

SAINT GEORGE AND
THE DRAGON

Once upon a time in the early days of the Christians, in the reign of the Emperor Diocletian, there was born in the province of Cappadocia, in Asia Minor, a beautiful baby boy, named George, who grew up to be a brave soldier and knight. Once when he was on a pilgrimage to the Holy Land he came to a town in the country of Libya where the people were living in great terror because a great dragon, with poisonous breath, had his home in a marsh outside the city walls. The monster had devoured their sheep and oxen, and the people were forced to shut themselves close inside their city and send out each day a sheep to satisfy the hunger of this dreadful dragon. At last not one sheep was left. Then the King ordered that each day two children, chosen by lot, should be sent out to the dragon. The people obeyed the King's order and from day to day arose the bitter cries of parents upon whose children the cruel lot had fallen. But one morning the lot fell upon Cleodolinda, the beautiful fifteen-year-old daughter of the King. He was in despair, for he loved his little daughter most tenderly. He offered all the gold in the treasury and half his kingdom if she should be spared. But the parents who had been obliged to sacrifice their children insisted that the King's daughter should be given to the dragon, and threatened to burn the King in his palace if he did not send her forth at once. The King pleaded for eight days longer to bid farewell to her. Then he sent her forth weeping, and arrayed her in royal robes, to die for her people. Walking timidly toward the terrible monster's den, along the path strewn thick with the bleaching bones of her former playmates, she suddenly heard the sound of hurrying horse's hoofs. She looked up, and there was a beautiful young knight in armor, on a milk-white horse, coming toward her with a gleaming spear, ready to do battle with any enemy that might cross his path. She cried, "Fly! fly for your life, Sir Knight!" But when he had heard her sad story, he said: "God forbid that I should fly! I will destroy this monster, your enemy, and deliver you through the power that lives in all true followers of Christ." Just then the dragon came forth, half flying and half crawling toward them, clashing his bronze scales with horrid noise. Cleodolinda again begged the knight to fly and leave her to her fate. But Saint George made the sign of the cross and rushed upon the monster. The struggle was fierce and long, for it was hard to strike through the dragon's bronze scales. But at last, with a blow like that of three strong men, Saint George pinned the dragon to the earth with his lance. Cleodolinda did not run away but, "with folded hands and knees full truly bent," the brave girl stood near her champion, who said: "Touch him and see how tame he is. See, even his poisonous breath is gone. It is the power of good over evil." Then he took the girl's rich girdle, bound it round the great dragon, and gave one end to her, telling her to lead the dragon into the city. So the girl who had obediently gone out to the dragon expecting him to devour her, obediently led the powerless creature over the fields he had laid waste and over the bleaching bones of the children he had devoured, and the meek monster followed her like a lamb toward the walls of the city where the people were gathered in terror. Saint George called out: "Fear not, only believe in the Christ through whose might I have overpowered your enemy, and I will destroy the dragon before your eyes." Then he took his sword and smote off the dragon's head, and all the people hailed him as their deliverer. But Saint George bade them give God the praise. He preached to them so earnestly that the King and princess and all the people became Christians. He would not take the gold the King offered him, but ordered that it be distributed among the poor. Then he bade them all adieu and rode away to do in other lands like noble deeds of loving service. So this champion of the weak became the patron saint of merry England, and only the bravest knight or soldier may wear the cross and be called a Knight of Saint George.

William J. Sly

THE DAUGHTER WHO HONORED HER MOTHER

(Book of Ruth)

Far away in the strange land of Moab a poor widow started to return to her own home in the land of Israel. Ruth and Orpah, her two daughters-in-law, the wives of her sons who had just died, wished to go with her, for they could not think of the poor, old, sad mother returning all by herself on that long journey. But after they had gone a little way, the old mother kissed them and said, "Go back to your home and native land!" So Orpah kissed her good-bye and returned, but Ruth clung to her mother-in-law and said: "Entreat me not to leave thee and return from following after thee; for whither thou goest I will go; and where thou lodgest I will lodge; thy people shall be my people, and thy God my God; where thou diest will I die, and there will I be buried. Nothing but death shall part thee and me." Ruth knew that where Naomi was going she would be poor, and that they would have to work hard, but she loved this old mother too much to leave her. Soon they saw the hills and then the houses of Bethlehem, Naomi's home. They settled down in that little town, but were so poor they did not know how to get even food enough to eat. The time of year had come when the farmers were beginning to cut the barley—the harvest-time. It was the custom in that land to allow poor people to go into the fields and gather up the loose ears of barley that were left by the reapers; and Ruth went to glean a little food for herself and her mother. She happened to go into the field of a rich man named Boaz. By and by when Boaz came to see how the reapers were getting on, he saw Ruth gleaning, and asked his reapers who she was. They told him that she was Naomi's daughter-in-law, just come from Moab. Then Boaz called her to him and told her that she was welcome to glean in his fields all through the harvest. He said: "I have heard all about your goodness to Naomi. May you be fully rewarded by Jehovah, the God of Israel, under whose wings you have come to take refuge." At dinnertime Boaz told her to sit down with the reapers, who gave her food and drink. She ate all she wished, and still she had some left, which in the evening she took home with her, with the barley she had gleaned, to Naomi. At the end of the barley harvest, this great and good rich man, Boaz, fell in love with Ruth, and she became his wife. The old mother, Naomi, went to live with them in their large and beautiful house, and she never was in want again. When a little son came to them, Ruth called his name Obed, and when he grew to be an old man, he was the grandfather of King David. So Ruth, the gleaner, who was kind and loyal to her mother-in-law, became the great-grandmother of the greatest King of Israel.

William J. Sly

THE COYOTE AND THE INDIAN FIRE-BRINGER

One cold winter's day, long, long ago, when the Coyote was the friend and the counselor of the Indian, a Boy of one of the tribes was ranging through a mountain forest with a big, gray Coyote. The poor Indians ran naked in the snow or huddled in caves in the rocks, and were suffering terribly in the cold. The Boy said, "I am sorry for the misery of my people." "I do not feel the cold," said the Coyote. "You have a coat of fur," said the Boy, "and my people have not. I will hunt with you no more until I have found a way to make my people warm in the winter's cold. Help me, O counselor." The Coyote ran away, and when he came back, after a long time, he said, "I have a way, but it's a hard way." "No way is too hard," said the Boy. So the Coyote told him they must go to the Burning Mountain to bring fire to the people. "What is fire?" asked the Boy. "Fire is red like a flower, yet not a flower; swift to run in the grass and destroy, like a beast, yet not a beast; fierce and beautiful, yet a good servant to keep one warm, if kept among stones and fed with sticks."

"We will get the fire," said the Boy. So the Boy and the Coyote started off with one hundred swift runners for the far-away Burning Mountain. At the end of the first day's trail they left the weakest of the runners to wait; at the end of the second day the next stronger, and so for each of the hundred days; and the Boy was the strongest runner and went to the last trail with the Coyote. At last the two stood at the foot of the Burning Mountain, from which smoke rolled out. Then the Coyote said to the Boy, "Stay here till I bring you a brand from the burning. Be ready for running, for I shall be faint when I reach you, and the Fire-spirits will pursue me." Up the mountainside he went. He looked so slinking and so small and so mean, the Fire-spirits laughed at him. But in the night, as the Fire-spirits were dancing about the mountain, the Coyote stole the fire and ran with it fast away from the Fire-spirits who, red and angry, gave chase after him, but could not overtake him. The Boy saw him coming, like a falling star against the mountain, with the fire in his mouth, the sparks of which streamed out along his sides. As soon as the Coyote got near, the Boy took the brand from his jaws and was off, like an arrow from a bent bow, till he reached the next runner, who stood with his head bent for running. To him he passed it, and he was off and away, and the spiteful Fire-spirits were hot in chase. So the brand passed from hand to hand and the Fire-spirits tore after each runner through the country, but they came to the mountains of the snows ahead and could not pass. Then the swift runners, one after the other bore it forward, shining starlight in the night, glowing red in the sultry noons, pale in the twilight, until they came safely to their own land. There they kept the fire among the stones and fed it with sticks, as the Coyote had said, and it kept the people warm.

Ever after, the Boy was called the Fire-bringer, and the Indians said the Coyote still bears the mark of fire, because his flanks are singed and yellow from the flames that streamed backward from the firebrand that night in the long ago.

Adapted from "The Basket Woman," by Mary Antrim

COURAGE

It is easier to pluck a thistle than it is to plant a flower. All I ask of those who knew me best is to remember that I plucked a thistle and planted a flower wherever the flower would grow.

In my youth I was fortunate in having a loving mother, a kind and considerate father who instilled into my young mind that I would pass through this world but once and if I were permitted to complete life's journey, the road to happiness would not be found through the primrose path by the easiest way but like the Christian in *Pilgrim's Progress*, I must fortify myself with courage and self-sacrifice to pass through the Slough of Despond in order to reach the mountain peaks of Hope and Happiness.

So, all my life, I have tried to pluck a thistle and plant a flower wherever the flower would grow with the thought in mind that to live in the hearts of those we leave behind is not to die.

Abraham Lincoln

Love's Sacrifice

O thou who camest from above,
   The pure, celestial fire to impart,
Kindle a flame of sacred love
   On the mean altar of my heart,
There let it for thy glory burn
   With inextinguishable blaze.
And trembling to its Source return,
   In humble prayer and fervent praise.

Jesus, confirm my heart's desire
   To work, and speak, and think for thee,
Still let me guard the holy fire,
   And still stir up thy gift in me,
Ready for all thy perfect will
   My acts of faith and love repeat,
'Till death thy endless mercies seal,
   And make my sacrifice complete.

Charles Wesley
1707–1788

The Bridge Builder

An old man, going a lone highway,
Came, at the evening, cold and gray,
To a chasm, vast, and deep, and wide.
Through which was flowing a sullen tide.
The old man crossed in the twilight dim;
The sullen stream had no fears for him;
But he turned, when safe on the other side,
And built a bridge to span the tide.
"Old man," said a fellow pilgrim, near,
"You are wasting strength with building here;
Your journey will end with the ending day;
You never again must pass this way;
You have crossed the chasm, deep and wide —
Why build you the bridge at the eventide?"

The builder lifted his old gray head:
"Good friend, in the path I have come," he said,
"There followeth after me today
A youth, whose feet must pass this way.
This chasm, that has been naught to me,
To that fair-haired youth may a pitfall be,
He, too, must cross in the twilight dim;
Good friend, I am building the bridge for him."

Will Allen Dromgoole

FOLLOWING JESUS

They were all going along the road. Someone said to Jesus, "I will follow you any place you go."

Jesus answered, "The foxes have holes to live in. The birds have nests to live in, But the Son of Man has no place to rest his head."

Jesus said to another man, "Follow me!"

But the man said, "Lord, first let me go and bury my father."

But Jesus said to him, "Let the people who are dead bury their own dead! You must go and tell about the kingdom of God."

Another man said, "I will follow you, Lord, but first let me go and say good-bye to my family."

Jesus said, "Anyone who begins to plow a field but keeps looking back is of no use in the kingdom of God."

Luke 9:57-62 ICB

RESULTS OF PERSEVERANCE

In earthly wars, not everyone who fights shares the spoils. The gains of war are commonly put into a few pockets. The common soldier, who endures most of the hardship, usually goes away with little of the profit. He fights to make a few that are great yet greater, and is often discharged without enough to pay for the cure of his wounds. But in Christ's army, the only soldier who loses is the one who runs away. Every faithful soldier receives a glorious reward, which is spelled out in this phrase, "having done all, to stand." To stand implies these things:

It means "to stand conquerors."

An army, when conquered, is said to fall before its enemy, and the conqueror stands. At the end of this spiritual war, every Christian shall stand a conqueror over his vanquished lusts and Satan who headed them. Though the Christian enjoys many sweet victories here over Satan, still the joy of his conquests is interrupted by fresh alarms from the rallied enemy. He wins a victory one day, only to be confronted with still another battle on the next. And often, even his victories send him from the conflict bleeding. Though he repulses the temptation at last, yet the wounds his conscience receives in the fight cast a shadow on the glory of the victory.

For your eternal comfort, Christian, you can look forward to a day when there will be a full and final decision in the quarrel between you and Satan. You will see your enemy's camp completely scattered, with not a weapon left in his hand to use against you. You will tread upon the very fortresses from which he fired so many shots. You will see them dismantled and demolished, until there is not one corruption left standing in your heart for the devil to hide himself in. On that glorious day, the enemy who has made you tremble will be trampled under your feet.

William Gurnall

BE OF GOOD CHEER

A young boy was playing left field in a Little League game when a man yelled over the fence, "Hey son, who's winning?"

The little boy replied, "We are!"

"What's the score?"

"They're beating us 23-0."

"They're beating you 23-0?" The man was confused. "I thought you said you were winning."

"Oh, we are," explained the little boy. "You see, we ain't come to bat yet!"

It was easy for the disciples to quit. The one in whom they had placed their hopes was dead.

And we are sometimes tempted to quit. . . . Jobs don't go well. There is strife in our marriage. A doctor's diagnosis may not be good. Children do not become what we dreamed they would be.

Remember—it may be the eighth inning, but there's still the ninth. Today may be a dark Saturday, but tomorrow is Easter.

Maxie Dunnam

THE THING OF MOST WORTH

There was once a very important King who was growing quite old and gray. He had three sons, Prince Proud and Prince Charming and Prince Great Heart, all fine, good boys and for that reason it was hard to decide which should wear the crown when the King should not need it any longer.

Prince Proud was very important and he stood up very straight as he held a standard beside his father's throne on days of the council. His eyes were blue and his golden hair was bright and shining in the sunlight. Prince Proud would make a very good King indeed, the court thought.

Prince Charming was very kind and thoughtful of the happiness and comfort of everyone. Dressed in a red velvet suit and with his brown head held high, he went about the throne room upon the days of the council saying pleasant words to all the lords and ladies. It seemed to everyone that Prince Charming would make a very gracious King.

Prince Great Heart was the youngest and smallest of the three princes and sometimes it seemed to his father, the King, that he was strangely different from his brothers. Prince Great Heart once changed his beautiful blue silk suit for the brown cotton smock of a little plough boy because, as he explained, he wanted to see if the plough boy's clothes would fit him. On the days of the King's council which, everyone knew, were the most important days of all, it was often hard to find Prince Great Heart. He would be off with the little court pages, or talking to the plough boy, or watching the ways of the brown squirrels and red foxes that lived in the forest about the palace. "Little, wandering Great Heart will not make a King at all," said certain of the court, and at times his father wondered if, after all, they were not right.

One morning at sunrise when the dew was like diamonds on the roses in the palace garden and the towers and battlements glistened with sunshine gold, the King called his sons into his bed chamber.

"I am growing older each day, my Princes," he said, "and less able to rule over my kingdom. I must choose which of you will take my place. To do this I will test you. Do you start out at once,

Prince Proud and Prince Charming and Prince Great Heart and, taking with you only your day's food, search the Kingdom for the Thing of Most Worth. What this is you must discover, but whichever of you finds it and brings it to me shall wear my crown and rule in my stead."

So the three Princes started out to find the Thing of Most Worth. They were all greatly puzzled, for they had not the slightest idea what it would be. Prince Proud searched in the great city which was the capital of the kingdom, for he thought that everything of importance must be stored there.

Prince Charming went to the neighboring castles, for he thought that his friends would tell him how to find the Thing of Most Worth.

But Prince Great Heart went away from the city and away from the court and down to the fields where the little plough boy lived, and no one could tell what he was thinking, for Great Heart's thoughts were very strange.

It was a long and a busy day for the three Princes. When night came they hurried back to the palace where the King waited for them on his great, shining throne. They knelt down at his feet, first, and then he bade them rise.

"Who has brought me the Thing of Most Worth?" the King asked of the three.

"I have," shouted Prince Proud.

"No, I have," smiled Prince Charming.

But little Prince Great Heart did not say a word.

"We shall see," said the King. "Show me." He pointed to Prince Proud who drew from beneath his cloak a gold casket. Opened, the light of a hundred precious stones flashed red and white and violet.

"It is the treasure of the oldest miser in your kingdom," explained Prince Proud. "He instructed me to bring it to you."

The King took the casket of jewels and laid it aside, shaking his head sorrowfully. Then he motioned to Prince Charming.

The prince came forward and held up a precious bit of filmy lace. It was as soft as a cloud and as fine as a spider's web and as beautiful in pattern as a snow flake.

"One of the Princesses made it with her own hands," Prince Charming said. "She will wear it when she is presented to you. I could find nothing more valuable."

The King touched the lace gently, but he shook his head again. "What has my little Great Heart brought?" he asked.

"Nothing," said Prince Great Heart, holding out two empty hands. "I had no time to search. I stopped at the plough boy's farm and helped him all day with the ploughing, for his father is sick and furrows must be dug for the wheat." Two tears welled up in Great Heart's eyes.

"Come nearer, Great Heart," said the King. He took Great Heart's little hand in his. In the palm was a hard, rough spot where he had held a plough handle all day.

"Prince Great Heart has brought me the Thing of Most Worth," said the King as he touched the spot tenderly. "He brings to the kingdom the marks of unselfish work."

So Great Heart wore the King's crown and although, at first, it was very large for him, everyone said that this did not matter in the least for he would soon grow to it.

Fannie E. Coe

DUST UNDER THE RUG

There was once a mother, who had two little daughters; and, as her husband was dead and she was very poor, she worked diligently all the time that they might be well fed and clothed. She was a skilled worker, and found work to do away from home, but her two little girls were so good and so helpful that they kept her house as neat and as bright as a new pin.

One of the little girls was not very strong, and could not run about the house; so she sat still in her chair and sewed, while Minnie, the sister, washed the dishes, swept the floor, and made the home beautiful.

Their home was on the edge of a great forest; and after their tasks were finished the little girls would sit at the window and watch the tall trees as they bent in the wind, until it would seem as though the trees were real persons, nodding and bending and bowing to each other.

In the spring there were birds, in the summer the wild flowers, in autumn the bright leaves, and in winter the great drifts of white snow; so that the whole year was a round of delight to the two happy children.

But one day the dear mother came home sick; and then they were very sad. It was winter, and there were many things to buy. Minnie and her little sister sat by the fireside and talked it over, and at last Minnie said, "Dear sister, I must go out to find work, before the food gives out." So she kissed her mother, and, wrapping herself up, started from home. There was a narrow path leading through the forest, and she determined to follow it until she reached some place where she might find the work she wanted.

As she hurried on, the shadows grew deeper. The night was coming fast when she saw before her a very small house, which was a welcome sight. She made haste to reach it, and to knock at the door.

Nobody came in answer to her knock. When she had tried again and again, she thought that nobody lived there; and she opened the door and walked in, thinking that she would stay all night.

As soon as she stepped into the house, she started back in surprise; for there before her she saw twelve little beds with the bedclothes all tumbled, twelve little dirty plates on a very dusty table, and the floor of the room so dusty that I am sure you could have drawn a picture on it.

"Dear me!" said the little girl, "this will never do!" And as soon as she had warmed her hands, she set to work to make the room tidy.

She washed the plates, she made up the beds, she swept the floor, she straightened the great rug in front of the fireplace, and set the twelve little chairs in a half-circle around the fire; and, just as she finished, the door opened and in walked twelve of the strangest little people she had ever seen. They were just about as tall as a carpenter's rule, and all wore yellow clothes; and when Minnie saw this, she knew that they must be the men who kept the gold in the heart of the mountain.

"Well!" said the men, all together, for they always spoke together and in rhyme:

> "Now isn't this a sweet surprise?
> We really can't believe our eyes!"

Then they spied Minnie, and cried in great astonishment:

> "Who can this be, so fair and mild?
> Our helper is a stranger child."

Now when Minnie saw the men, she came to meet them. "If you please," she said, "I'm little Minnie Grey; and I'm looking for work because my dear mother is sick. I came in here when the night drew near, and—"

Here all the men laughed, and called out merrily:

> "You found our room a sorry sight,
> But you have made it clean and bright."

After they had thanked Minnie for her trouble, they took white bread and honey from the closet and asked her to eat with them.

While they sat at supper, they told her that their housekeeper had taken a holiday, and their house was not well kept, because she was away.

They sighed when they said this; and after supper, when Minnie washed the dishes and set them carefully away, they looked at her often and talked among themselves. When the last plate was in its place they called Minnie to them and said:

> "Dear little maiden, will you stay
> All through our helper's holiday?
> And if you faithful prove, and good,
> We will reward you as we should."

Now Minnie was much pleased, for she liked the kind little people, and wanted to help them, so she thanked them, and went to bed to dream happy dreams.

Next morning she was awake with the chickens, and cooked a nice breakfast; and after the miners left, she cleaned up the rooms and mended their clothes. In the evening when the men came home, they found a bright fire and a warm supper waiting for them; and every day Minnie worked faithfully until the last day of the housekeeper's holiday.

That morning, as Minnie looked out of the window to watch the little men go to their work, she saw on one of the window panes the most beautiful picture she had ever seen.

A picture of fairy palaces with towers of silver and frosted pinnacles, so wonderful and beautiful that as she looked at it she forgot that there was work to be done, until the cuckoo clock on the mantel struck twelve.

Then she ran in haste to make up the beds, and wash the dishes; but because she was in a hurry she could not work quickly, and when she took the broom to sweep the floor it was almost time for the miners to come home.

"I believe," said Minnie, aloud, "that I will not sweep under the rug to-day. After all, it is nothing for dust to be where it can't be seen." So she hurried to her supper and left the rug unturned.

Before long the miners came home. As the rooms looked just as usual, nothing was said; and Minnie thought no more of the dust until she went to bed and the stars peeped through the window.

Then she thought of it, for it seemed to her that she could hear the stars saying:

"There is the little girl who is so faithful and good"; and Minnie turned her face to the wall, for a little voice, right in her own heart, said:

"Dust under the rug! dust under the rug!"

"There is the little girl," cried the stars, "who keeps home as bright as star-shine."

"Dust under the rug! dust under the rug!" said the little voice in Minnie's heart.

"We see her! we see her!" called all the stars joyfully.

"Dust under the rug! Dust under the rug!" said the little voice in Minnie's heart, and she could bear it no longer. So she sprang out of bed, and, taking her broom in her hand, she swept the dust away; and lo! under the rug lay twelve shining gold-pieces, as round and as bright as the moon.

"Oh! oh! oh!" cried Minnie, in great surprise; and all the little men came running to see what was the matter.

Minnie told them all about it; and when she had ended her story, the men gathered lovingly around her and said:

> "Dear child, the gold is all for you,
> For faithful you have proved and true;
> But had you left the rug unturned,
> A nickle was all you would have earned.
> Our love goes with the gold we give,
> And oh! forget not while you live,
> That in the smallest duty done
> Lies wealth of joy for everyone."

Minnie thanked them for their kindness to her; and early next morning she hastened home with her golden treasure, which bought many things for the dear mother and little sister.

She never saw the miners again; but she never forgot their lesson, to do her work faithfully; and she always swept under the rug.

Maud Lindsay

THE BOY HERO OF HOLLAND

Once there was a good boy who had a kind-hearted mother. One afternoon she said: "Here, Peter, are some cakes I want you to take to the poor old blind man who is very ill, and who lives a mile and a half away from town. If you go quickly and do not stop to play, you will be home before it is dark." Peter took the cakes to the poor old blind man, who said, "You are a kind-hearted boy; thank your mother for me." Light-hearted because he had made the blind man happy, Peter was walking home when suddenly he noticed a little stream of water trickling through the great bank on the side of the road. This was in Holland, where much of the land is below the level of the sea, and where dikes are built by the people to keep back the sea. Every boy in Holland knows the danger of even a small leak in the dike. Peter understood at once that this tiny stream would soon make a large hole and the whole city would be flooded. In a moment he saw what he must do. He climbed down the side of the dike and thrust his chubby little hand and finger into the tiny hole and stopped the flowing of the water. Then he cried out for help, but no one heard him; no one came to help. It grew dark, and cold; he was hungry; his arm ached and it began to grow stiff and numb. He shouted again: "O mother! mother!" But his mother thought Peter must be spending the night with the blind man, and did not know of his danger. Peter thought how warm and cozy all at home were sleeping in their beds, and he said to himself, "I will not let them be drowned!" So that good boy stayed there all night long, holding back the water. Early next morning, a minister on his way to visit the sick, heard a groan, saw the boy, and called out to him, "What is the matter, my boy? Are you hurt? Why are you sitting there?" When Peter told him what he had done, the minister said, "I will hold my hand there while you run quickly to the town and get help." Very soon men came and repaired the leak in the dike, but all knew that Peter, by his courage and faithfulness, had saved the town of Haarlem that night.

THE GERMAN PATRIOT AND THE BARLEY-FIELDS

Once there was a terrible battle in Germany, and thousands of soldiers were scattered over the country. A captain who had many men and horses to feed was told by his colonel to get food from the farmers near-by. The captain walked for some time through the broad valley, and at last knocked at the door of a small cottage. A man, old and lame and leaning on a stick, opened the door. "Good morning," said the captain. "Will you please show me a field where my soldiers can cut grain for our army? We cannot pay for it." The old man led the soldiers through the valley for about a mile, when they saw a field of rich barley waving in the breeze.

"That is just what we want," said the captain. "No, not yet," said the old man; "follow me a little farther." After some time they came to a second field of barley. The soldiers got off their horses, cut the grain, tied the sheaves, and rode away with them. Then the captain said to the old man, "Why did you make us come so far? The first field of barley was better than this one." "That is true, sir," answered the old man, "but it was not mine!"

Adapted from "Ethics for Children," by E. L. Cabot

THE JAPANESE AND THE EARTHQUAKE

Once in far-away Japan there lived a rich man who owned a large ranch—not of alfalfa, or wheat, or other grain—but of rice. One afternoon he stood looking over his large fields of rice, saying, "What a rich man this great harvest makes me!" Suddenly he felt an earthquake and saw that the waves of the sea were running away from the land and rolling far out. He knew that it would only be a little while before the waves would return in a great flood, which would overflow the little strip of land along the seashore, in the valley below the high plain on which his ranch was situated, and all the people in the little village would be drowned. It was a holiday and the people in their merrymaking and fun and laughter had not noticed the earthquake. The rich man cried to his servants, "Bring torches! make haste! set fire to the rice!" Then he and his servants set on fire stack after stack of the rice. In a moment the flames and smoke rose high, the big bell from the village pealed the fire-signal, and all the boys and girls and men and women ran up the hill as fast as they could to see the fire, and to try to save the rice-crop of the rich man. When they saw him setting fire to his rice, they shouted, "Look, he is mad; he is setting fire to his rice." "Look!" shouted the old man. They looked and saw the raging and surging waves of the sea come rolling in. They looked again a few moments later and saw nothing but the straw which had been the thatched roofs of their homes tossing on the waters and their whole village blotted out by the sea. "That is why I set fire to my rice," said the old Japanese. "If I had not done that you would have all been drowned in those waves!" He stood among them almost as poor as any of them, but he had the consciousness that by the sacrifice of his fortune he had saved four hundred lives that day.

Adapted from "Gleanings in Buddha-fields," by L. Hearn

PROMISES TO KEEP

It is eight o'clock at night, the hour when a hush settles over the house. I tuck Robert and John into their twin beds in the bedroom they share, a cozy, protected, south-facing room with a fine view of the woods. I sit on the edge of the beds—first one, then the other, in order to give equal time—quietly conversing until sleep overtakes them. There are a few final questions as they struggle to keep their eyes open. They want to know where snakes live in the winter and whether a balloon set adrift will float all the way to outer space. Then the eyelids flutter, the mouths open slightly, the breath comes soft and deep, and I am left with the darkness and the peace.

But tonight, instead of stillness, I hear singing coming from the woodshed and the clunking and thudding of wood on wood. Jeff, my oldest son, home from college for a short recess, is loading up logs to bring into the house.

"Whose woods these are I think I kno-o-w," he sings with the robustness that amateurs often affect when they think no one is listening. It is Robert Frost's poem set to music, a choral arrangement that was part of his secondary-school repertoire. Only now it isn't boys in blue blazers on one side and girls in white dresses on the other; there is no teacher, baton in hand, to monitor his performance—only Jeff alone, working in the darkness and singing for the pure fun of it.

I go to the window and look out. The waist-deep snow in the back yard, refreshed nearly every few days with a new layer, has drifted halfway up the side of the woodshed. In the light of a ponderous, ripe moon, it is incandescent. Tonight there is no wind to transform the shadows of the woodland trees into wild, leaping monsters equipped with grabbing arms. The only darkness that plays across the board white expanse is the web-like shadow of the smoke from the woodstove, billowing in soft puffs from the chimney. It drifts in delicate waves, gracefully twisting, turning, changing direction with each new waft of air.

"He will not see me sto-o-pping here/ To watch his woods fill up with sno-o-w." It has been a long time since I have heard such a performance from Jeff, and it surprises me that his voice no longer cracks and breaks when he tries for the high notes. It is a man's voice now, melodious and assured. What is even more surprising, though, is that his song beats out a rhythm for this job that he has hated for all of his growing-up years. How many battles there were about how much wood he should bring, and when he should bring it, and how it should be stacked.

In the darkness, with the music around me, I remember his 10-year-old face — white, frightened, the eyes stricken and wide — as he came flying back from the shed without the wood he should have gotten in the afternoon. "I heard a noise out there," he said, breathless. "It is so dark I can't see but . . ." he struggled to control his voice and the tears, ". . . I think it is a rat!" We got the flashlight. Richard put his arm around Jeff's shoulders as they went out the door together. In a little while, he was back with the wood and a little embarrassed smile.

It is hard to teach children to work, to accept responsibility for doing often unpleasant but necessary jobs like swabbing the floor, taking out the trash, or scouring the bathroom sink. Even the best of children harbor the hope that if they ignore the job long enough or do it wrong often enough, parents will give up and leave them to their play. More often than not, it takes more time and energy to supervise a reluctant child than to do the job yourself. But if we do not teach our children "living skills" and gradually increase their responsibilities as they grow into independent adults, we fail them as parents. I look at my two sleeping boys and wonder how many more times we will have to illuminate dark corners, before they will sing songs, too.

"The woods are love-ly, dark and deep,/ But I have pro-o-mises to keep." The song is traveling now. Jeff is returning to the house. I go downstairs to meet him as he backs through the doorway, his arms loaded.

"You were singing, Jeff," I say, and tease him with a smile that lets him know that the irony of the situation has not escaped me.

"Don't fall over dead when I tell you this, Mom," he confides, "but I don't hate getting the wood anymore. In fact, I think I like it." The thumping of the split logs dropping into the woodbox punctuates his sentence. Behind his glasses, somewhere deep in his eyes, there is a little twinkle. I smile at him. We understand each other.

Later, lying in bed, when half-sleep makes the mind wander like the shadows of woodsmoke, I think of his joyful song. I picture the notes as written music, trailing their little tails behind them, escaping easily through the open shed door, invading the silence of the woods, drifting up and up into the moonlit sky like hundreds of runaway balloons. Maybe they will, as the children imagine, float all the way to the stars.

"Whose woods these are I think I kno-o-w," Jeff's voice sings in my mind. And just as sleep slips over my thoughts, I think that I know too.

Mary E. Potter

MR. RHOADES'S NEIGHBORHOOD

The moment I set eyes on the house, I knew it was "home" as I'd always wanted it to be. The place was no mansion—it occupied a narrow piece of land only 37 feet wide—and the neighborhood was gradually becoming surrounded by pockets of urban decay. But sitting in the heart of St. Louis, the house was more than a century old and overlooked the Mississippi River. So I bought it.

Having recently been widowed, I was advised by friends and family to "do something you always wanted to do." As a lifetime lover of the city and its history, I decided to restore this house.

After the final papers were signed, however, I soon realized the property had a few problems. A four-foot-high stack of old bricks leaned against the back fence, the fireplaces didn't work, the lock on the front door was inoperable and there was no walk from the front porch to the street.

How am I going to find workmen? I worried. *Especially ones I can trust and afford?*

One morning a neighbor said to me, "You'd better get acquainted with Mr. Rhoades. He does everything for everybody in the neighborhood. There's nothing he can't fix."

The next day the doorbell rang. "I'm Rhoades," said the apparition on my doorstep. "I hear you want to talk to me."

For a moment I was speechless. His was the high, quavering, uncertain voice of an old, *old* man. Slight and toothless, with a full head of white hair, he was wearing ill-fitting work clothes, and he leaned on a crutch to support his right leg. I guessed he was between 75 and 80 years old. This was the neighborhood savior?

Suddenly my hope for a perfectly restored property vanished. "Thank you for coming by," I said. "I was wondering whether you would cut my grass this summer."

Quickly I learned he was not just old, he was grumpy. "Well, if I can get to it, I will," he said. "I can't do everything, you know. C'mon out here. I wanna show ya somethin'." I followed as he hobbled down the front steps into the side yard.

"First," he began, "ya gotta do somethin' about this yard. The rainwater can't get through this brick fence. In the winter it freezes over so you can skate on it. In the summer the ducks stop by for a swim."

I didn't know whether to laugh or cry. Although I was fairly fit for a 55-year-old, my physical exercise usually ended with plugging in the toaster. "Ya gotta level the whole yard, so the rain runs down through drain tile," he continued, "which ya gotta put in that fence so the water can go out in the street."

"Mr. Rhoades," I said, "I can't do that. Being a commercial artist takes up most of my day. Besides, I don't understand what you're talking about."

It was as if I were speaking to the brick fence. "Yup," he insisted, "ya better get it done."

Suddenly I lost patience. "If you know all about it," I snapped, "then why don't *you* do it!" I expected an angry reply, but instead he looked satisfied: he'd gotten the job. I'm still not sure how it happened.

The next day he started cutting dead limbs off the tall oak trees that shaded the house. No, he said, he didn't need his crutch when he was up in the trees—he had ropes and straps left over from felling trees many years ago in the Colorado mountains.

The Colorado mountains? Who is this old man? I wondered. His speech revealed origins in the rural South, but when I asked neighbors, they knew little about him. Mr. Rhoades did not encourage questions.

Each day he'd save cut branches so I could see how many "hundreds" he'd removed before chopping them into kindling for himself and the neighbors. "You must tell me how much you charge for all this work," I said three times that first week.

"I don't charge nothin'," he replied. "People pay me what they can."

"Mr. Rhoades," I said firmly, "I can't pay you more than $50 per week. Please don't do more than that amount."

"I can't quit in the middle of a job just because there ain't any money," he replied. End of conversation.

Slowly the yard was leveled, and truckload after truckload of debris disappeared. Gradually it dawned on me that this was no catch-as-catch-can landscape design. Mr. Rhoades had formulated its needs with loving care long ago.

"Wha'cha gonna do with all them bricks back there by the fence?" he asked one evening.

"Well," I said, "I'm thinking of getting someone to build a circular brick patio as big as the lot will accommodate."

Mr. Rhoades looked surprised, and he didn't come around for a week. Did he think I intended to hire someone else? I had merely wanted to find out if he would offer to do it himself. I certainly didn't want to hurt his feelings.

Then one afternoon when I returned from work, there was a 24-foot circle of tamped-down sand. A center of bricks was set in it, with some spliced to fit neatly into the round. I was full of admiration. "This is just what I wanted," I said.

"Well," Mr. Rhoades answered, "I don't do nothin' till it's figured out in my head. The work itself don't take no time at all."

He was right. Within three days all the bricks were laid and the patio was bordered with cobblestones. Two days later he added brick drains that carried rainwater through tile under the fence to the street. I was amazed by the artistic arrangement of the elements, and told him.

"Well," he said, puzzled, "ain't that the way it's supposed to be?"

I found out that Mr. Rhoades considered it his duty to inspect the work of others—including any plumber or electrician who appeared in the neighborhood. If he judged the man incompetent, Mr. Rhoades invited him to leave. We could then call someone capable—whose work would also be inspected.

Soon I began to notice a certain uniformity in the greenery within this two-block area of town. The lawns were lush, the flowers perky, the trees and bushes healthy. I learned why one afternoon when I found Mr. Rhoades planting flowers around my patio.

"They're from Miss Scott's yard," he told me. "She had too many and they were crowded, so I took them. Then I put some of your leftover bricks around her flower beds. She had so many flowers I had to plant some at the teacher's house on the corner.

And the teacher had extra evergreens that look just fine in front of Miss Scott's house. There's more harm than good done if things go to waste."

By this time we were having regular consultations after work. Gradually he began to talk of people who had influenced his life. He was especially proud of his father, who had instilled in him his ironclad rules of right and wrong.

"I was nine and he was 73 when he died," Mr. Rhoades said. "Once I'd made me a little wagon with red wheels. When I showed it to him, I said I coulda done a better job if I'd had somethin' on wagons to go by. But he didn't think so. 'Son,' he said, 'don't ever mix up books and brains. Books will tell you how to do somethin'. But with brains you can figure it out yourself. That's a real good wagon.'" Mr. Rhoades took a deep breath. "I ain't never forgot that."

Later he talked about his "graduation" from fourth grade, about having to leave home to go to work, about living under a bridge in Chicago when he was 12 and selling newspapers for two cents a copy, about sending money to his mother each month until her death. He told of his prideful habit of quitting a job upon being promoted rather than deal with any paper work that would expose his poor education. He never lacked a job, he said, and he never kept one he knew he could not handle.

As the year went on, I came to realize you didn't ask Mr. Rhoades to do a job—you mentioned that something was broken or not quite right; then he would fix it when he got to it. So when a little shower made the porch gutters overflow like Niagara Falls, I ventured they needed cleaning. As usual, he said nothing. Then one afternoon he called, "C'mon over here. I wanna show ya somethin'," and headed toward the porch.

"Now look up there," he said. "Can't ya see? There ain't nothin' wrong with your gutters. The whole porch has sagged six inches. That's what's wrong."

Six inches? My immediate visions were of building contractors, carpenters and painters, along with accompanying bills. How much would a job like this cost? Two thousand dollars—if I was lucky?

"Don't do nothin' yet," he instructed. "I'll be back."

A few days later I heard the familiar rumbling of Mr. Rhoades's pickup truck. Inside were stout pieces of lumber, heavy rope, and pulleys and jacks. There were nails and hammers and saws of all sizes. "I think I got it figured out," he said.

The next four days were like exhibition time at the zoo. People filed through the yard to observe this old man with the crutch gradually lift the entire porch. With an occasional "Howdy," Mr. Rhoades was enjoying his audience. Oh, no, help wasn't necessary, he assured one and all. It wasn't that big a job.

Never seeming to exert himself, he adjusted pulleys here, tightened ropes there, raised and lowered jacks in a series of mysterious moves. He measured and sawed, removed rotted lumber and replaced it with solid pieces. Then he painted it white and trimmed it in Williamsburg gray. When I came out to look at the finished product, I couldn't believe my eyes. The porch could never have looked this good in all its years.

"I ain't never done nothin' like that before in my life," Mr. Rhoades told me, a rare, broad smile creasing his face. He leaned on his crutch, viewing his latest accomplishment with pride. Then he presented me with his bill—for $163.78. It was for materials only, he said, since I had already paid him for the week.

As I stood admiring Mr. Rhoades's work, I realized that here was the stuff from which America had been built. These were the very qualities that enabled our forefathers to face the staggering challenge of a vast wilderness. With freedom to find their own solutions, everlasting willingness to try new ideas, independence of mind, they built great cities and towns for those who followed them.

A month later I received a certificate of merit for the most beautifully restored property in the area. I showed it to Mr. Rhoades—for it truly belongs to him—but he was unimpressed, telling me he did not waste his time on such things. Today it is proudly displayed in my front window for all to see.

Last year Mr. Rhoades celebrated his 90th birthday. He is a bit slower now, his crutch having given way to two canes. Still, it was only grudgingly that he finally stopped doing the neighborhood handiwork. But before passing the torch to new workmen—all roughly one-third his age—he made one key demand. If they wanted to work in the neighborhood, they had to do so under his critical eye.

The workers agreed, although they knew they had no choice—since we neighbors would have had it no other way. Even today, I still find myself pausing now and then, imagining that I hear a high, quavering voice ring out loudly: "C'mon over here, I wanna show ya somethin'."

Pat Walsh

THE LITTLE BAKER

All the children were glad when the Little Baker came to town and hung the sign above his little brown shop:

Thanksgiving Loaves to Sell

Each child ran to tell the news to another child, until soon the streets echoed with the sound of many running feet, and the clear November air was full of the sound of happy laughter, as a crowd of little children thronged as near as they dared to the Little Baker's shop, while the boldest crept so close that they could feel the heat from the big brick oven, and see the gleaming rows of baker's pans.

The Little Baker said never a word. He washed his hands at the windmill water spout and dried them, waving them in the crisp air. Then he unfolded a long spotless table, and setting it up before his shop door, he began to mold the loaves, while the wondering children drew nearer and nearer to watch him.

He molded big long loaves, and tiny round loaves; wee loaves filled with currants, square loaves with strange markings on them; fat loaves and flat loaves and loaves in shapes such as the children had never seen before, and, always as he molded, he sang a soft tune to these words:

> Buy my loaves of brown and white,
> Molded for the child's delight.
> Who forgets another's need
> Eats unthankful and in greed;
> But the child who breaks his bread
> With another, Love has fed.

By and by the children began to whisper to each other.

"I shall buy that very biggest loaf," said the Biggest Boy. "Mother lets me buy what I wish. I shall eat it alone, which is fair if I pay for it."

"Oh," said the Tiniest Little Girl, "that would be greedy. You could never eat so big a loaf alone."

"If I pay for it, it is mine," said the Biggest Boy, boastfully, "and one need not share what is his own, unless he wishes."

"Oh," said the Tiniest Little Girl, but she said it more softly this time, and she drew away from the Biggest Boy and looked at him with eyes that had grown big and round.

"I have a penny," she said to the Tiniest Little Boy "and you and I can have one of those wee loaves together. They have currants in them, so we shall not mind if the loaf is small."

"No, indeed," said the Tiniest Little Boy, whose face had grown wistful when the Biggest Boy talked of the great loaf. "No, indeed, but you shall have the bigger piece."

Then the Little Baker raked out the bright coals from the great oven into an iron basket and he put in the loaves, every one, while the children crowded closer, with eager faces.

When the last loaf was in, he shut the oven door with a clang so loud and merry that the children broke into a shout of laughter.

Then the Little Baker came and stood in his tent door, and he was smiling; and he sang again a merry little tune to these words:

> Clang! clang! my oven floor:
>   My loaves will bake as oft before;
>   And you may play where shines the sun
>   Until each loaf is brown and done.

Then away ran the children, laughing and looking back at the door of the shop where the Little Baker stood and where the raked-out coals, bursting at times, cast long red lights against the brown walls; and as they ran they sang together the Little Baker's song:

> Clang! clang! my over floor:
>   My loaves will bake as oft before.

Then some played hide-and-seek among the sheaves of ungarnered corn, and some ran gleefully through the heaped-up leaves of russet and gold for joy to hear them rustling. But some, eager, returned home for pennies to buy a loaf when the Little Baker should call.

So the hour passed, till, above the sound of the rustling corn, and the sounds of all other voices, the children heard the Little Baker's call:

> The loaves are ready, white and brown,
> For every little child in town.
> Come buy Thanksgiving loaves and eat,
> But only Love can make them sweet.

Soon all the air was filled with the sound of swift-running feet, as the children flew, like a cloud of leaves blown by the wind, in answer to the Little Baker's call. When they came to his shop they paused, laughing and whispering, as the Little Baker laid out the loaves on the spotless table.

"This is mine," said the Biggest Boy, and laying down a silver coin he snatched the great loaf and ran away to break it by himself.

Then came the Impatient Boy, crying:

"Give me my loaf. This is mine, and give it to me at once. Do you not see my coin is silver? Do not keep me waiting."

The Little Baker said never a word. He did not smile, he did not frown, he did not hurry. He gave the Impatient Boy his loaf and watched him, as he, too, hurried away to eat his loaf alone.

Then came others crowding and pushing with their money, the strongest and rudest gaining first place; and snatching each a loaf, they ran off to eat without a word of thanks, while some very little children looked on wistfully, not able even to gain a place. All this time the Little Baker kept steadily on, laying out the beautiful loaves on the spotless table.

A Gentle Lad came, when the crowd grew less, and, giving all the pennies he had, he bought loaves for all the little ones; so that by and by no one was without a loaf. The Tiniest Little Girl went away hand in hand with the Tiniest Little Boy to share her wee loaf, and both were smiling; and whoever broke one of those smallest loaves found it larger than it had seemed at first.

But now the Biggest Boy was beginning to frown.

"This loaf is sour," he said angrily.

"But is it not your own loaf," said the Baker, "and did you not choose it yourself, and choose to eat it alone? Do not complain of the loaf since it is your own choosing."

Then those who had snatched the loaves ungratefully and hurried away, without waiting for a word of thanks, came back.

"We came for good bread," they cried, "but those loaves are sodden and heavy."

"See the lad there with all those children. His bread is light. Give us, too, light bread and sweet."

But the Baker smiled a strange smile.

"You chose in haste," he said, "as those choose who have no thought in sharing. I cannot change your loaves. I cannot choose for you. Had you, buying, forgotten that mine are Thanksgiving loaves? I shall come again; then you can buy more wisely."

Then these children went away thoughtful.

But the very little children and the Gentle Lad sat eating their bread with joyous laughter, and each tiny loaf was broken into many pieces as they shared with one another, and to them the bread was as fine as cake and as sweet as honey.

Then the little Baker brought cold water and put out the fire. He folded his spotless table and took down the boards of his little brown shop, and packed all into his wagon and drove away, singing a quaint tune. Soft winds rustled the corn and swept the boughs together with a musical chuckling. And where the brown leaves were piled the thickest, making a little mound, sat the Tiniest Little Girl and the Tiniest Little Boy eating their sweet currant loaf happily together.

From THE CHILDREN'S STORY GARDEN
Collected by a Committee of the Philadelphia
Yearly Meeting of Friends. © *1920*
by J. B. Lippincott Company.

THE FLOWER THAT LIVES
ABOVE THE CLOUDS

Long ago when the flowers first woke to life on earth, each chose where it would live.

"I will cover the ground and make the bare soil warm with green blades," cried the grass.

"I will live in the fields and by roadsides," laughed the daisy.

"I, too," echoed the buttercup, the cornflower, the poppy, and the clover.

"Give me the ponds and the lakes," the water lily called.

"And let us have the streams and the marshes," begged the irises, cowslips, and Jacks-in-the pulpit.

"We love the shaded, ferny woodland spots," lisped the shy forget-me-nots and wood-violets.

"And we wish to live in gardens," declared the rose, the pansies, the sweet williams, and the hollyhocks.

"I love the warm dry sun—I will go to the sandy desert," said the cactus. So all places except the bare ridges of high mountains were chosen. To these, no flower wished to go.

"There is not enough food there!" the daisy explained.

"There is not enough warmth! There is not enough food!" all decided. "It is so bare and chilly! Let the gray moss go and cover the rocks," they said.

But the moss was loath to go.

"When one cannot live without moisture, warmth, nourishment—when one must live in a garden, surely the bleak places of the mountains must do without flowers! How foolish it would be to try to make the ragged, bare mountaintops lovely! Let the gray moss go—he has not yet chosen!"

So the gray moss went up the high mountains because he was told to go. He climbed over the bare rocks beyond the places where forests ceased to grow. All was desolate and silent up there.

Up higher and higher crept the gray moss. It went even above the clouds where the ragged rocks were covered with ice and snow.

There it stopped short in amazement, for it found a quiet star-shaped flower clinging to the crags and blossoming! It was white like the snow around it, and its heart was of soft yellow. So cold was it up there that the little flower had cased its leaves in soft wool to keep warm and living in the bleakness.

"Oh!" cried the gay moss, stopping short. "How came *you* here where there is no warmth, no moisture, no nourishment? It is high above the forests, high above the clouds! I came because I was sent. Who are you?"

Then the little starry flower nodded in the chill wind. "I am the edelweiss," it said. "I came here quietly because there was need of me, that some blossom might brighten these solitudes."

"And didn't anyone tell you to come?"

"No," said the little flower. "It was because the mountains needed me. There are no flowers up here but me."

The edelweiss is closer to the stars than the daisy, the buttercup, the iris, or the rose. Those who have courage, like it, have found it high above the clouds, where it grows ever gladly. They call it Noble White — that is its name, edelweiss! Love, like the edelweiss, knows not self-sacrifice.

From THE CHILDREN'S STORY GARDEN
Collected by a Committee of the Philadelphia
Yearly Meeting of Friends. © *1920*
by J. B. Lippincott Company.

A Garden of Virtues
Copyright Notices and Permissions